DEPARTMENT OF ENG
UNIVERSITY OF MICHIGAN
ANN ARBOR

A STUDY
OF
CHROMIUM PLATING

RICHARD SCHNEIDEWIND
Assistant Investigator
Department of Engineering Research
University of Michigan

ENGINEERING RESEARCH BULLETIN
No. 10
September, 1928

A VIEW OF THE EXPERIMENTAL PLATING LABORATORY AT THE UNIVERSITY OF MICHIGAN

Since this picture was taken during the installation of the laboratory, only a portion of the equipment is shown, but an idea may be gained of the size of the work that can be handled.

TABLE OF CONTENTS

INTRODUCTION	7–9
Objects of the Bulletin	8
Plan of Presentation	8–9
PART I. A NON-TECHNICAL ACCOUNT OF CHROMIUM PLATING FROM CHROMIC-ACID BATHS	11–18
Properties of Chromium	11–13
The Process of Plating	13–18
PART II. STUDIES ON THE PROCESS OF ELECTRODEPOSITION OF CHROMIUM	19–75
Introduction	19
Section 1. The Effects of Bath Composition, Nature of Anodes, and Plating Conditions on the Quality and Yield of Metallic Chromium	19–43
Section 2. The Effects of Bath Composition, Nature of Anodes, and Plating Conditions on Anode Behavior	43–47
Section 3. The Effects of Bath Composition, Nature of Anodes, and Plating Conditions on the Ultimate or Equilibrium Bath Composition	47–64
Section 4. Miscellaneous Notes on Control of Plating and on Nature of the Deposits	64–73
Conclusions Drawn from the Research	73–75
PART III. A REVIEW OF THE SCIENTIFIC AND PATENT LITERATURE ON THE ELECTRODEPOSITION OF METALLIC CHROMIUM	77–94
PART IV. A BIBLIOGRAPHY	95–121
PART V. APPENDICES	122–141
Appendix A. A Summary of the History of the Development of Chromium-Plating Processes	122–126
Appendix B. Tables of Data on Original Research	126–141

ACKNOWLEDGMENTS

This bulletin is a summation of the results of a research program on chromium plating financed by The Detroit Edison Company. Its preparation has been aided by the encouragement and counsel of Mr. C. F. Hirshfeld, Chief of Research of that company, at whose suggestion the work was undertaken. Thanks are due to Professors E. M. Baker and A. H. White of the Department of Chemical Engineering for their kind assistance and friendly criticism. Acknowledgments are also made to Messrs. S. F. Urban and R. C. Adams, Jr. for their invaluable aid in the experimental work. A portion of the material has appeared in the Transactions of the American Electrochemical Society and has been reprinted here with the permission of that Society.

SYNOPSIS

A previous Bulletin entitled "A Study of Patents Dealing with the Electrodeposition of Chromium" has been published by the Department of Engineering Research. The information presented therein has not been included in the present bulletin, which deals largely with original data on the subject of chromium plating. The experimental work done in the course of the investigation has led to the following general conclusions:

I. In order to obtain smooth, bright plates these conditions must be maintained:
   1. A chromic-acid concentration between 150 and 600 grams per liter, preferably between 250 and 300 grams per liter.
   2. A sulphate concentration, relative to the chromic acid concentration and expressed as the ratio by weight $\frac{Cr^{VI}}{SO_4}$, of between 40 and 60, preferably, 50.
   3. A trivalent chromium concentration under 15 grams per liter, preferably as close to 0 as possible.
   4. A temperature over 15°C. This is especially imperative for thin deposits.
   5. A combination of current density and temperature resulting in a cathode current efficiency of 13 per cent. Current efficiency has been shown to be a function of the logarithm of the current density.

II. In order to favor a low rate of anode corrosion:
   1. A low sulphate concentration must be maintained.
   2. Too high a temperature should not be used.
   3. In the case of iron or steel anodes too low an anode current density, under 2.0 amperes per square decimeter must not be used.
   4. Anode material must be used whose inherent solubility is not great. Lead is best, iron next best.

III. Under fixed bath composition, anodes, and plating conditions the concentration of trivalent chromium of the solution comes to equilibrium. The factors favoring a low trivalent chromium concentration are:
   1. A low sulphate concentration.

2. The inherent nature of the anode material probably due in turn to the magnitude of the oxygen overvoltage on that anode material.
3. A low temperature.
4. A low anode current density.
5. Continuous electrolysis rather than alternate application and cessation of current.

IV. Miscellaneous Studies.
1. Further work is necessary for the development of completely satisfactory methods for chemical analysis and plant control.
2. Heavy chromium deposits exhibit voids and cracks.

In the review of the literature and bibliography the development of chromium plating has been traced from 1852 to the present time.

A STUDY OF CHROMIUM PLATING

No other factor, perhaps, has so directly influenced the growing interest in chromium plating as has the existence of a highly organized automobile industry, continuously, methodically seeking materials which may prolong the appearance and useful life of a motor car. In the field of corrosion-resisting coatings such as zinc, copper, and nickel, the demands of the automobile industry have brought about standardization of processes and great improvement in quality of product. For example, nickel-plated steel can now be expected consistently to resist a salt spray test for a period of fifteen hours,—even fifty hours is not unusual,—whereas plating such as had been done for decades up to the period just at the close of the World War, would scarcely withstand three or four hours. Improvements of the same order have been effected in the cases of zinc, cadmium, and similar coating metals.

But even the best nickel plating will tarnish and lose its luster. In the days when varnish finishes were applied to motor cars this matter was of little importance since there was no demand for a material which could retain its appearance longer than the rest of the car. But with the advent of pyroxylin lacquers better metal coatings were imperative. Chromium plating attracted the automobile industry because it is smooth, brilliant, and resistant to tarnish. In heavy layers its extreme hardness makes it resistant to frictional wear. It is, therefore, easy to see why so great an interest should be manifest in chromium.

Although the industry was ready for a metal such as chromium and although by 1920 sufficient research[44]* had been accomplished to develop solutions virtually the same as those in general use today, yet the development of chromium plating as an industrial process has been comparatively slow. This apparent lethargy on the part of the industry can not be ascribed to unreliable directions published in the literature but has been due to other causes. Some of these were the relative impurity of chemicals commercially obtainable, the necessity for unusual and careful control of the process, and the confusion in the patent situation. Many papers of little scientific value have been published giving misleading information which was probably the result of incomplete or careless work. These factors all

---

*The superscripts refer to the number of the reference in the bibliography in the fourth section of the bulletin. Where the article has not been of sufficient general interest to abstract it, the superscript will consist of a letter instead of a number.

[44] G. J. Sargent. Trans. Am. Electrochem. Soc. 37: 479–496 (1920).

contributed to the many difficulties which were encountered in trying out chromium plating methods on an industrial scale. Among the outstanding work published after 1920 a paper by Haring and Barrows[99] in 1927 substantiating the findings of Sargent has extended his work and has offered explanations for the inconsistent results obtained by various workers. Since then there is apparent an encouraging trend toward standardization of process and of results.

Objects of the Bulletin.

In this bulletin there is given an account of research work on chromium plating done at the University of Michigan during the years 1927 and 1928. A large amount of important information has also been compiled from the scientific and patent literatures. It is hoped that such an assembling of material on the subject may to a measure aid in opening a way to the wider use of chromium plating.

Plan of Presentation.

In preparing this bulletin an attempt has been made to present it in a useful form to two classes of readers, to executives and engineers interested in chromium plating in a general way and to electrochemists. Hence, in order that the information may be given clearly and completely the following general form has been used:

First there is presented a non-technical account of electrodeposited chromium and commercial methods for its preparation. This has been given in as elementary language as possible and without unnecessary details.

Second is a detailed account of the original research done at the University of Michigan during the years 1927 and 1928. The effects of bath composition, nature of anodes, and plating conditions upon the results are taken up. Some of this material has already been printed as separate articles and is reprinted here in order to make a complete story of the research. Some points dealing with commercial processes have been the result of the writer's personal observations.

Third is a review of the scientific and patent literatures on the subject. Outstanding articles have been discussed and freely quoted.

Following this in the fourth part is the bibliography proper. No attempt at completeness has been attempted for the period after about 1922 when a

---

[99] Bureau of Standards. Technologic Paper 346.

large number of rather popular articles have been published, most of which merely repeat statements found elsewhere. Due to the plan of writing, all of the information presented in a given article may not be abstracted in detail under the reference but may be found in the review of the literature or as a part of the discussion in the main body of the paper. Proper acknowledgment, however, has been made in all cases.

The fifth part of the bulletin contains a summary of a review of the literature arranged in tabular form and also contains tables of data on the experimental work.

PART I

A NON-TECHNICAL ACCOUNT
OF
CHROMIUM PLATING FROM CHROMIUM ACID BATHS

PART I

A NON-TECHNICAL ACCOUNT OF CHROMIUM PLATING FROM CHROMIC ACID BATHS

The adoption of chromium plating as a commercial process has proceeded with surprising and increasing rapidity in the last five years. Manufacturers everywhere have found the public quite ready to accept the bluish brilliance of chromium as a standard of elegance and good taste. Coatings of this metal have been used to decorate radiator shells, bumpers, and headlamps on automobiles, plumbing fixtures, household appliances, and even jewelry. Not only is chromium attractive for its luster, but unlike other metals used for the same purpose its brightness is not dimmed by weather, nor is it tarnished by atmospheric conditions, nor by the smoke and fumes ordinarily found in big cities. In the case of automobile fittings especially, chromium plating is applied also as means of protecting the base metal, usually steel, from rusting. A very thin coating, even a few hundred-thousandths of an inch in thickness, when applied over the usual nickel plate, will increase the resistance to corrosion two or threefold. These qualities have been responsible for the increasing popularity of chromium plating.

PROPERTIES OF CHROMIUM PLATE

Electrodeposited chromium is a bluish metal which, if properly applied, has a brilliant luster quite similar to that of polished platinum. Chromium in thin layers is used to improve the appearance of a surface and also to prevent corrosion of the under-metal. In thick layers it is used to increase resistance to wear. Chromium plating on steel without intermediary coatings of copper, nickel, or other metals, however, is of little value in protecting against corrosion due to the extreme thinness of the deposit and its tendency to be porous. Ollard[84] made quite an extensive study of the corrosion resistance of multiple coatings such as nickel-chromium, cadmium-copper-chromium, copper-chromium, and many others on steel.

[84] Metal Industry (London) 27: 70–79 (1925).

Certain of these combinations are described in various patents.[a] Ollard found that a simple chromium plate did not appreciably protect the steel from rusting, whereas the multiple coatings improved greatly the effectiveness of the coating. Baker and Pinner[104] found that unless the undercoating or coatings were of moderate thickness the plate would corrode rapidly. This was found especially true where the undercoating was copper. Baker and Pinner also found that increasing the thickness of the chromium deposit over a nickel-copper-nickel undercoating up to a certain point increased the resistance to corrosion proportionately. This was due to the fact that a heavier coating is less apt to be porous than a thinner one. Beyond this optimum thickness the rust resistance of the plated piece decreased in a way that had not been anticipated. They found on examination that the chromium deposit had formed microscopic cracks which made it of little protective value. Grant and Grant[103] published some very interesting pictures of the structure of heavier layers of electrodeposited chromium which exhibited cracks visible even at fairly low magnification.

Chromium is not only useful as a protective covering against rust: it is used also in thick layers to impart greater durability and wear resistance to moving parts of machinery and like equipment. Examples of this type of application are found in automobile parts, such as wrist-pins and steering-knuckles, brake parts, and in stamping-dies, extrusion-dies, roller-faces, and plug-gages.[102]

There are two characteristics which distinguish it from other metals and fit it peculiarly for such service. These are its hardness and its smoothness. According to the mineralogists' scale it has a hardness of 9, which means that only corundum and diamond can scratch it. Payne[b] gives the following table of comparative scratch hardness which will give a fair idea of the hardness of chromium as compared with other metals:

Chromium	2000
Case hardened steel	1950
Steel shafting	750
Swedish iron	408
Cobalt	625
Bronze	244
Babbitt	208
Copper	78

---

[a] U. S. P. 1614303 (1927).
U. S. P. 1578254 (1926).
U. S. P. 1615585 (1927).
U. S. P. 1651278 (1927).
U. S. P. 1587293 (1926).
[104] Jour. Am. Soc. Auto. Engrs. March (1928).
[103] Trans. Am. Electrochem. Soc. 53: Preprint (1928).
[102] Am. Soc. Steel Treating 12: 921–945 (1928).
[b] U. S. P. 1600961 (1926).

As for the "smoothness" of chromium, its coefficient of friction is extremely low,—so low that greaseless bearings[b] have been made in which the sliding surfaces carry a fairly heavy coating of the metal. It is doubtful, however, whether this procedure could be used commercially in very many places.

The greatest defect in thick coats of chromium is a result of its metallographic structure. This leads to a pronounced tendency for the metal to crack when struck a blow or when a varying load is applied to it. Some of this tendency to crack can be ascribed to inherent brittleness. Treatments such as heating or heating in a vacuum to remove occluded hydrogen, formed during the plating process, have been suggested and may be of some value.

On polishing a cross sectional specimen of heavy chromium plate, and examining it under a microscope there will be found a large number of voids in the deposit. In some cases these voids will happen to be so aligned that a crack or fissure extends all the way down to the base metal. Although usually the holes are not so connected it is obvious nevertheless that such a material, rather brittle to begin with, can not withstand shock.

There is undoubtedly some correlation between plating conditions and the number of voids in the resultant deposit. This, however, has not yet been fully investigated. A few isolated tests by the author would lead to the conclusion that the hotter the bath, or in other words the more rapidly the metal is built up, the more pronounced the voids which will result in the deposit.

THE PROCESS OF ELECTRODEPOSITION OF CHROMIUM

Electroplating in general is accomplished by passing an electric current from one electrode to another through a bath containing in solution the metal which it is desired to deposit. For example, in nickel plating, a nickel rod is used as the positive electrode, while the object to be plated becomes the negative electrode. These two poles are immersed in a bath of nickel sulphate or other suitable salt of nickel and an electric current is passed through the solution. The current causes the nickel rod to dissolve gradually and replenish the bath from which nickel is simultaneously being deposited upon the surface to be plated. In this manner a cycle is set up: nickel rods, called anodes, and current are constantly supplied to the process, and in return nickel is obtained as a coating upon the objects hung in the bath.

The deposition of all metals follows very definite laws. Normally a

[b] Loc. cit.

certain amount of electric current will transfer a definite amount of metal from anode to cathode, the article to be plated. If less metal is deposited than should be theoretically obtained, it is said that the cathode current efficiency is low. Cathode current efficiency can, therefore, be expressed as the ratio between the amount of metal deposited and the amount theoretically calculated and is reported in per cent. Anode current efficiency is the ratio beween the amount of anode actually dissolved and the theoretical amount.

Anodes.

In most plating processes new metal is supplied to the bath in the form of anodes which dissolve in the plating solution at approximately the same speed as that at which metal is being deposited from the solution. There are only two well known exceptions to this procedure, which are found in the electrodeposition of platinum and in that of chromium. Here, insoluble anodes are made use of, and the bath is replenished by means of metallic salts.

Soluble anodes of chromium metal, however, are not entirely unknown. In 1923, Wolff[66] advocated the use of such anodes in chromic-acid plating baths, and gave a method for their production by means of pressing powdered chromium into desired shapes and sintering. Soon afterward Coignard[68] described the successful use of ferro-chromium in chromic-acid baths, although Sargent[44] had not found them satisfactory. Schwartz[53] favored both of these materials.

Important objections, however, to the use of soluble anodes in chromic-acid baths have recently been raised by Haring and Barrows[99] and by Watts,[100] who found that the current efficiency of chromium and ferro-chromium anodes is much greater than the cathode current efficiency. This means that during electrolysis chromium goes into solution at a more rapid rate than that at which metal is depositing out from the solution. Hence, the concentration of chromium, especially the trivalent chromium, builds up rapidly and the bath becomes inoperable.

Only in solutions of divalent and trivalent salts of chromium have chromium anodes been found entirely satisfactory. But even in baths of this

[66] D. R. P. 422461 (1925).
[68] Fr. P. 571447 (1924).
[44] Trans. Am. Electrochem. Soc. 37: 479–496 (1920).
[53] Trans. Am. Electrochem. Soc. 44: 451–463 (1924) also U. S. P. 1589988 (1926).
[99] Bureau of Standards Technologic Paper 346.
[100] Trans. Am. Electrochem. Soc. 52: 177–185 (1927).

nature insoluble anodes have been described. Moeller and Street,[16] Cowper-Coles,[22] Carveth and Mott[31] and others used lead anodes in solutions of chrome alum or chromic chloride.

Hambuechen[c] fully realized the fact that with soluble anodes the bath would rapidly become too rich in chromium. In order to surmount this obstacle he patented an ingenious process for using insoluble anodes of lead in conjunction with auxiliary soluble anodes of chromium. When the chromium concentration fell below a certain predetermined figure, the auxiliary anodes were introduced into the bath and were removed when the bath composition was satisfactory.

In the majority of installations insoluble anodes are used. The researches of Watts[100] definitely narrowed the selection of possible materials to two: iron or lead. If lead anodes are used, the bath will be maintained in a very good condition because trivalent chromium formed during electrolysis is readily reoxidized by lead anodes. Some grades of lead, however, corrode in such a manner that adherent patches of lead chromate are formed which exert a detrimental effect upon the plate. Iron anodes on the other hand always remain clean. They permit, however, a greater accumulation of trivalent chromium in the bath than lead anodes. Moreover iron goes into solution. The more pure the iron the slower will be the rate of solution. Iron in the bath increases its resistance and thereby increases both the power necessary for plating and the attendent power costs. These factors must be considered in making a choice of anode materials. If properly taken care of, lead anodes are preferable.

Tanks.

The plating bath may be contained in a lead-lined wooden vat, or in a glass-lined steel tank but a common procedure is to use a steel tank in which the joints are lapped and welded inside and out. Steel and iron become passive in chromic acid and are but very slightly attacked. As has been pointed out before, sheet-lead or sheet-steel anodes may be hung in the bath or, in the case of a steel tank, the tank itself may be connected anodically. Heating and cooling coils are usually installed in order that the temperature may be controlled readily.

[16] B. P. 18743 (1899).
[22] Chem. News 81: 16 (1900).
[31] Jour. Phys. Chem. 9: 231-256 (1905).
[c] U. S. P. 1544451 (1925).
[100] Loc. cit.

The deposition of chromium is attended by a copious evolution of gas,—hydrogen and oxygen mixed with a spray containing chromic acid. This fume is very irritating to the mucous membranes; exposure over a long period of time leads to bad head colds, nose bleed and even ulceration in the nasal passages. For this reason fume ducts are generally installed very near the surface of the bath. Exhausting fans pull the fumes directly across the solution and downward. In earlier equipment it was attempted to pull the fumes upward but due to the density of the spray this method did not function satisfactorily. European installations sometimes are equipped with traps to collect the spray, which is returned to the tank periodically.

The Bath.

The chromium plating bath has as its main constituent chromic acid. Its function in the bath is two-fold: to conduct the electric current, and to act as the source of supply of chromium. During the operation of plating, chromic acid must be added from time to time.

A solution of chromic acid alone will not yield commercially valuable deposits of metal. It is essential that small quantities of sulphate or its equivalent be added in amounts about one per cent as great as that of the chromic acid used. The most convenient way of adding sulphate is through the use of sulphuric acid; chromium sulphate, sodium sulphate or any such material, however, can be substituted. Of these substances, however, more than one per cent must naturally be added. Carveth and Curry laid the foundations of this study, which was completed by Sargent, Fink, and Haring and Barrows. Substances functioning similarly to sulphates can be substituted, but no industrial concern is doing so.

If there is a deficiency of sulphate, the resulting deposit will contain areas of a brown hydroxide of chromium. As the amount of sulphate is increased, the quality of the plate is improved. When too great an amount of sulphate is present, good plate can be obtained only in a very narrow range of plating conditions. Still more sulphate makes the bath entirely inoperable.

The plating bath is usually quite strong; the chromic acid concentration in a recommended formula is about 250 grams per liter (32 ounces per gallon), the sulphate concentration 2.5 grams per liter ($\frac{1}{3}$ ounce per gallon). A stronger or weaker solution may be used, but the constituents must be in about the same relative proportions. Many baths contain other constituents either added intentionally or formed during use. Most substances of this nature, however, are detrimental rather than beneficial to the deposit.

Process of Deposition.

The cathode, the article to be plated, must be carefully cleaned of all grease, oil, and oxide. The grease and oil are removed by cleaning in a hot solution of alkalis, preferably with the aid of electric current in which case the piece to be plated is made the negative pole. Some foreign workers do not believe cleaning to remove grease a necessary step and they depend largely upon the detergent effect of the chromic-acid plating solution. Oxide is removed by pickling in acid; in the case of copper and brass, a solution of sodium cyanide works admirably. After it is rinsed, the piece is immersed in the chromic-acid plating bath, connected to the negative side of the circuit, and the current is applied.

In plating with nickel, silver, copper, or almost any other metal, if a small current is applied, deposition takes place slowly; if a large current is applied, deposition is rapid. The amount of plate formed is dependent upon the total amount of current supplied.

Chromium deposition is a much more complicated process. If a very low current density is used, the current merely reduces the chromic acid to trivalent chromium without any deposition of metal whatever. Current density is current per unit area and is usually expressed as amperes per square foot or amperes per square decimeter. As the current density is increased, a point is reached where suddenly an evolution of hydrogen is noticed at the cathode. Upon examination it will be found that, in addition to reducing chromic acid as before and liberating hydrogen, the current also has brought about the deposition of chromium. Only a very small fraction, under 5 per cent of the current at this stage actually is used in metal deposition. The plate is generally milky in appearance. Increasing the current density increases the current efficiency and the resulting deposit is brilliant. If put on a buffed surface, the plate will be so bright that no subsequent buffing is necessary. Increasing the current density still farther so that the current efficiency rises above 20 per cent results in a gray, matte deposit which in thick layers may crack and peel badly. There is, therefore, a range of current densities which will produce good plate. Certain metals, such as copper and brass, when used as cathode exhibit a comparatively wide range; other metals such as nickel and iron a narrower one.

Changing the temperature of deposition shifts this range. For example, at room temperature with a given solution good deposits can be obtained on copper between 20 and 80 amperes per square foot (2.2 and 8.8 amperes per square decimeter); at 60°C., between 70 and 600 amperes per square foot (7.7 and 66 amperes per square decimeter).

It will be found that, although the range of current densities producing good deposits increases with the temperature, the current efficiencies of the deposition remains nearly the same. That is, good plate for decorative purposes will be obtained between 5 and 20 per cent current efficiency regardless of the temperature. If thick deposits are desired a current density and temperature combination to give about 13 per cent current efficiency will form a bright, smooth plate with the minimum tendency toward treeing. A detailed study of these conditions will be taken up in the more technical account of chromium plating in the second part of this bulletin.

If the bath contains other things in addition to the essential chromic acid and sulphate or its equivalent, unfavorable conditions will result. For example, the formation and accumulation of trivalent chromium leads to increased resistivity in the bath. It also greatly contracts the plating-range already described. Dissolved iron also increases the resistivity of the solution. Other effects are not yet fully known.

Bright chromium surfaces are obtained by plating on bright under coatings. It is easier to obtain fine finishes by plating on a buffed undercoat of a metal like nickel than upon buffed copper. Dull chromium can, however, be buffed by using a special buffing compound although this procedure is generally uneconomical and is unnecessary.

The necessity for control is very great in chromium plating. In best installations there will be found thermostatic temperature control, recording thermometers, accurate ammeters, good fume exhausters, and there will be some provision made for a periodic chemical analysis of the bath. There is, however, no great measure of uniformity in the quality and extent of the control methods at the present time.

PART II

THE PROCESS OF THE ELECTRODEPOSITION OF CHROMIUM

PART II

THE PROCESS OF THE ELECTRODEPOSITION OF CHROMIUM

The problems in the electrodeposition of metallic chromium from chromic-acid plating baths can be conveniently studied with a fair degree of completeness by a consideration of research along three main lines. Although most of the results presented in this part of the bulletin were obtained in this investigation yet all of the work presented, naturally, has not been done by any one investigator but has been compiled from many sources. These studies are as follows:

I. The effect of bath composition, nature of anodes, and plating conditions on the cathode deposit.

II. The effects of bath composition, nature of anodes, and plating conditions on anode behavior.

III. The effects of bath composition, nature of anodes, and plating conditions on the ultimate or "equilibrium," bath composition.

A brief consideration is given of the inherent characteristics of the deposits and of methods of analysis and control of chromic-acid plating baths. In phases of the subject where all of the work has been done by other investigators the problems are taken up in the section devoted to a review of the literature.

SECTION I. THE EFFECTS OF BATH COMPOSITION, NATURE OF ANODES, AND PLATING CONDITIONS ON THE CATHODE DEPOSIT

Essential Components of the Bath.

Although Geuther,[3] Bartoli and Papasogli,[9] and Placet and Bonnet[12] reported electrolytic deposition of metallic chromium from a solution of chromic acid, it has been found by careful experiment that chemically pure chromic acid will not behave in this manner except at prohibitive current densities, if at all. Carveth and Curry[32] found that the addition of a comparatively small amount of sulphuric, phosphoric, nitric, or other acid, or salts of these acids, would so alter the characteristics of a chromic-acid

---
[3] Liebig. Ann. 99: 314 (1856).
[9] Gazz. Chim. Ital. 37: 47 (1883).
[12] U. S. P. 526114 (1894).
[32] Jour. Phys. Chem. 9: 353–380 (1905).

bath that electrodeposition could occur readily. They correctly concluded that the success of earlier workers was due to impurities in the chromic acid. The investigations of Askenasy and Revai[42] and of Fink[81] have substantiated all of these conclusions.

Opposed to these findings, however, are the results of Salzer[36] and of Liebreich.[45] These investigators found that metal was deposited from a solution of chromic acid to which trivalent chromium had been added. They stated that compounds of lower valences of chromium could be added in the form of oxides or hydroxides or could be formed from the chromic acid by chemical or electrolytic reduction. They were probably influenced by the following two facts: in any solution from which chromium has been deposited, there will always be found a quantity of trivalent ion; if a cathode is rapidly withdrawn from such a bath without first interrupting the current, a film of chromous or chromic hydroxides will be found on the piece. These phenomena probably induced Sargent also to change from Carveth and Curry's bath containing chromic acid and sulphate ions to one containing not only chromic acid and sulphate, but also trivalent chromium ions. Haring's earlier work and Grube's were in agreement with this practice. Salzer and Liebreich on the other hand took the extreme position that the essentials of a good plating bath consisted of chromic acid and trivalent chromium and that no other materials need be present in the solution. In later works,[37,109] both of these investigators specified sulphates to assist in metal deposition although they maintained their original theoretical premises.

In order to choose from these various theories two rather simple tests were made in the present investigation.

Five hundred cubic centimeters of a solution of chemically pure chromic acid, 250 grams per liter, was partially reduced by systematic additions, in the cold, of chemically pure Merck's perhydrol, 30 per cent hydrogen peroxide. After each addition the solution was electrolyzed at room temperature. Even after the addition of 150 cubic centimeters of the reagent no metal could be electrodeposited at current densities up to 80 amperes per square decimeter. Trivalent chromium was prepared in this manner because ordinary "chemically pure" chromium hydroxide or carbonate may contain as much as 15 per cent of sulphate.

[42] Zeit. f. Elektrochemie 19: 362 (1913).
[81] U. S. P. 1581188 (1926).
[36] D. R. P. 221472 (1910).
[45] Zeit. f. Elektrochemie. 27: 94–110 (1921).
[37] D. R. P. 225769 (1910).
[109] Oberflächentechnik 5: 107 (1928).

Another five hundred cubic centimeters of a solution of chromic acid, 250 grams per liter, was digested with a few grams of barium sulphate for three days at 80°C. At the end of this time the solution upon electrolysis yielded metallic chromium, evidently due to the solution of a small amount of sulphate. This procedure was used because it did not introduce any appreciable amounts of soluble cations nor did it alter the acidity of the bath. Whether this last factor was important or not, was not known at the time, but it has been subsequently proved by Haring and Barrows[99] to be negligible. Salzer's and Liebreich's commercial successes were undoubtedly due to the use of impure chemicals; the trivalent chromium was not essential.

The exact function of this trace of acid radical has not yet been fully investigated; it is a problem closely bound up with the whole theory of the deposition of chromium from chromic acid.

In this connection not a great deal can be said because, although several theories have been advanced, there are many phenomena not completely explained by them. Carveth and Curry,[32] Müller,[94] Lukens[110] and others believe that chromium is deposited directly from the hexavalent state. Carveth and Curry suggest the existence of a chromium cation bearing six charges whose formation is favored by the presence of sulphates. Müller, on the other hand, postulates the deposition of metal from undissociated chromic acid behind a film of chromium chromate or oxide. This film he believes acts as a diaphragm. Due to the presence of sulphate the film is damaged and thus chromic acid can reach the cathode to be reduced there.

Liebreich,[45] and Sargent,[44] among others believe that deposition of metal is the final reaction of a series of reductions. Liebreich states that deposition takes place from a divalent ion behind a cathode film of chromous-chromic oxides or hydroxides.

In a similar manner Fink[81] says: "activated by the catalyst (sulphate ion), chromic acid . . . . undergoes reduction when current is passed, releasing a chromium ion in the field of attraction of the cathode." At the cathode, a "definite film of hydrogen" is maintained. Behind this protecting film, chromium is deposited as a metal. If the film is too thin the ion is oxidized before it can be deposited; if the film is too thick, the discharge of the chromium ion is prevented.

[99] Loc. cit.
[32] Loc. cit.
[94] Zeit. f. Elektrochemie. 32: 399–413 (1926).
[110] Trans. Am. Electrochem. Soc. 53: Preprint (1928) in the discussion.
[45] Loc. cit.
[44] Loc. cit.
[81] U. S. P. 1581188 (1926).

It has been demonstrated by many workers, especially in the fields of heat transfer and fluid flow, that the fluid adjacent to a solid surface is stationary regardless of the motion in the main body of that fluid. It is very probable, therefore, that in contact with the cathode there is a stationary film of solution whose composition, during electrolysis, is different from that in the main body of the bath. As the electrolysis proceeds the film tends to become depleted of ions. At the same time the composition of the main body of solution is remaining approximately constant due to convection currents. Thus a concentration potential is set up between the cathode side of the film and the main body of the plating bath. The composition of the layer at the cathode is governed by the equilibrium between the rate at which ions are deposited and the rate at which material enters the film by diffusion and electrical transfer. Cathode reactions depend upon the composition of the cathode film and hence upon the interchange of material between the film and the main body of the bath.

For this conception, a film of solid or colloidal chromium hydroxide or similar substance or of gaseous hydrogen need not be assumed. These substances are probably formed by other reactions occurring simultaneously with chromium deposition or as a secondary phenomenon but are not necessarily the cause of deposition. The liquid film is bound to exist, as does the similar film in heat transfer concepts, whether or not solid material or gas is liberated at the cathode-solution interface. Deposition of gas or precipitation of solids at the cathode, convection currents, temperature changes and like disturbances may tend to change the thickness of the film but do not at any time completely destroy it. When influences are brought to bear which thin the cathode film, new material some of which is highly oxidizing is brought up at a more rapid rate than before. In order to maintain the particular equilibrium of favorable solution concentration within the film, the effect of the increased tendency for diffusion into the film must be counteracted by an increased rate of depletion. This may be accomplished by increasing the current density.

It is not known why bright plate is obtained between certain current density limits from a solution of one composition and between others from a solution of a second composition. In all of the cases observed in this investigation bright plate, if at all obtainable, was deposited when the cathode current efficiency with respect to metal deposition was near 13 per cent. The current density necessary to produce this, however, may vary greatly with different baths. By changing conditions of plating or of solution composition, not only is the position of the bright plating range shifted but also the extent of the range is altered considerably. In some cases no bright plate at all is obtainable. It is most probable that the ratio of chromium to hydrogen ions (not molecular hydrogen) in the cathode film has a very profound influence upon the nature of the deposit. No quantitative information unfortunately is available on this subject. Some of the factors which tend to narrow the bright plating range have been found, however, to be as follows:

1. Low temperature.
2. Too high or too low a sulphate concentration.
3. Too high or too low a chromic acid concentration.
4. The presence of a substance like trivalent chromium.
5. Low hydrogen overvoltage on the cathode.

Another point still open to investigation is the matter of the function of the sulphate ion. It is a question whether it migrates to the anode as would normally be expected or whether a part, at least, forms a complex ion with chromium and travels to the cathode. Carveth and Curry suggest that a small portion of the chromic acid may behave as a hexa-acidic base which is neutralized by sulphuric acid and gives rise to the presence of a hexavalent chromium cation. Fink merely calls the sulphate a catalyst. Certainly some definite explanation must be found for the necessity of maintaining the sulphate, or similar ion, concentration within very narrow limits and for the changes in behavior of the bath resulting therefrom.

The Relation Between Current Density and the Yield of Metallic Chromium.

Early investigators noted that the current efficiency of deposition increased with the current density. Sargent made a quantitative study of this behavior and this was later extended by Haring.[82] Haring found that, for a given bath at a fixed temperature, there was a range of current densities between which bright plate was obtainable. Below the lower limit a sparse, milky deposit was formed; above the upper limit the plate was dull with a tendency to crack and peel if applied in heavy layers.

Hence it is apparent that data on the relation of current density to current efficiency are not novel. Yet, it was believed that further investigation from this standpoint would not be unnecessary repetition because the whole subject of bath composition must be developed from this angle.

The relative concentrations of chromic acid and sulphate ion necessary to produce the optimum plating bath has been worked out by many in-

[82] Chem. and Met. Eng. 32: 692, 756 (1925).

vestigators with fair agreement. By calculating this ratio as the ratio by weight of hexavalent chromium to sulphate, $\frac{Cr^{VI}}{SO_4}$, the figures are as follows:

INVESTIGATOR	$\frac{Cr^{VI}}{SO_4}$	CrO_3
		g./l.
Sargent[44]	57 ±	250–300
Schwartz[53]	57	250
Grube[48]	58	250
Pierce and Humphries[e]	45	240
Fink[81]	52	250 ±
Haring and Barrows[99]	53	250
Liebreich[109]	43.3	

[44] Loc. cit.
[53] Loc. cit.
[48] U. S. P. 1496845 (1924).
[e] U. S. P. 1545196 (1925).
[81] Loc. cit.
[99] Loc. cit.
[109] Oberflächentechnik 5: 105–107 (1928).

Some others, Hosdowich,[f] Appel,[g] etc., who suggested different ratios, did not take into consideration the sulphate impurity in the chromic acid. The well known bath of Grube, if prepared with ordinary commercial chemicals in the recommended proportions, will contain a $\frac{Cr^{VI}}{SO_4}$ ratio of around 48 or 50 rather than 58 because of the sulphate in chromium hydroxide. Hence in order to study most extensively a solution of optimum composition for commercial use, a $\frac{Cr^{VI}}{SO_4}$ ratio of 50 was decided upon arbitrarily.

The actual composition of the bath studied was 234 grams per liter of chromic acid and 4.3 grams per liter of potassium sulphate.

A steel tank 7.5 cm. (3 in.) in diameter and 15 cm. (6 in.) high was used as the anode. The cathodes were test strips about 1.5 cm. (0.6 in.) wide and 13 cm. (5 in.) long cut from thin sheet copper. These strips were highly buffed on one side. Only 7.0 cm. (2.7 in.) of their length actually was plated. For each strip of this size 1000 coulombs of electricity were used in plating.

The temperature of the bath was maintained by means of a manually

[f] B. P. 259118 (1926).
[g] U. S. P. 1590170 (1926).

operated electric heater. When it was desired to operate the bath below room temperature, a glass tube fashioned in the shape of a U, through which cold water was circulated, was placed in the solution.

After electrolysis, in order to determine the current efficiency, the plated strips were weighed, stripped of chromium in a cold 15-per-cent hydrochloric acid bath, dried, and reweighed. The difference in weight divided by the weight of chromium theoretically reduced from the hexavalent ion gave the current efficiency. This method proved, for the purposes of this paper, to be as satisfactory as the method of Carveth and Curry who deter-

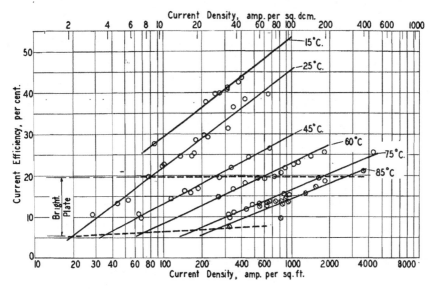

FIG. 1. Current Density-Current Efficiency Relationships. 234 g./l. CrO_3 and 2.42 g./l. SO_4. Copper Cathodes. Thickness of deposits 0.0007 mm. (0.00003 in.)

mined the weight of chromium deposited by means of the amount of hydrogen gas evolved by its solution in 15 per cent hydrochloric acid. Less accurate results were obtained by weighing the specimen before and after plating. This was due to etching of the copper cathode by the bath before current was applied, to etching of the portion extending out of the solution by spray during electrolysis. All three methods were tried before the first mentioned method was chosen.

A standard system was adopted for reporting the quality of plate: (1) Very sparse plate, covering the specimen only at the edges. (2) Incomplete plate, corresponding to "milky plate" of Haring. (3) Perfect plate, shiny over the entire surface. (4) Burnt plate.

Test strips were plated with chromium at 15°, 25°, 45°, 60°, 75°, and 85°C. (59°, 77°, 113°, 140°, 167°, and 185°F.), respectively. The results of current efficiency determinations are given in Tables 1 to 6 in the Appendix and graphically in Figure 1.

It was found that by plotting the current efficiencies against the logarithms of the current densities a straight line was obtained. In Fig. 1 the ordinate is current efficiency, which in this discussion will be called E. The abscissa is the logarithm of the current density, D. This was accomplished conveniently by plotting on semi-logarithmic paper.

It is apparent that the relationship between current density and current efficiency for metal deposition from these solutions is expressed by the equation

$$E = m \log D + b$$

where m is the slope of the line and b an intercept. This is reducible to the form

$$D^m = A \times 10^E$$

At 25°C., for example, for a solution containing nominally 250 g/l of chromic acid and 2.6 g/l of sulphate ion, that is, the ratio $Cr^{VI}/SO_4 = 50$, the slope can be read from the curve and is as follows:

$$\frac{45.4 - 21.8}{\log 1{,}000 - \log 100} = 23.6$$

A is a constant, which proves to be 2.5×10^{25} when D is expressed in amperes per square foot, and the expression simplifies to

$$D^{23.6} = 2.5 \times 10^{25 + E}$$

When D is expressed in amperes per square decimeter

$$D^{23.6} = 3.6 \times 10^{2 + E}$$

If desired, the slope of this line, m, can be plotted against temperature and the resulting expression will give, for a fixed bath composition, the relationship between the variables; current density, current efficiency, and temperature. Different amounts of sulphate affect the relationship markedly.

The bright plate ranges were obtained from data prepared from the experiments, and from qualitative tests made especially to determine the ranges.

It is to be noted that bright plate for a deposit up to 0.0007 mm. (0.00003 in.) in thickness or less is obtained between roughly current efficiency limits of 5 to 20 per cent on copper. Bright deposits of the same thickness on some other metals are obtained between narrower limits. Similarly, if heavy deposits are desired, 2 or 3 mm. (0.125 in.) thick, it has been found that plating conditions producing about 12 to 14 per cent current efficiency are the only ones which will deposit this plate without causing cracking or excessive treeing.

As an illustration of the results obtainable at 13-per-cent current efficiency

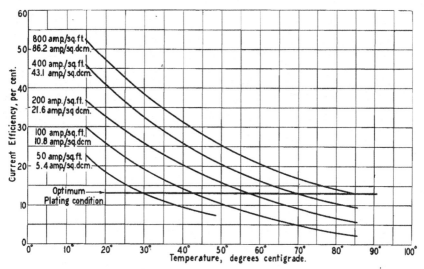

FIG. 2. Operating Chart for Bath Containing 234 Grams per Liter CrO_3 and 2.42 Grams per Liter SO_4. Ratio $\frac{Cr^{VI}}{SO_4} = 50$.

a deposit 2.5 mm. thick (0.10 in.) was deposited at 95 amp./sq. dm. (850 amp./sq. ft.) at 85°C. (185°F.) in about 35 hours. The deposit was bright, shiny, with a few small trees at the lower end. The specimen was a brass rod 6.5 mm. (0.25 in.) in diameter and 13 cm. (5 in.) long.

Figure 2 sums up these data in a form usable to a plater. It is presented according to the method of Haring, with current efficiency plotted against temperature. In the figure itself are drawn iso-current-density lines. The best conditions of current density and temperature to give bright deposits are indicated by the line representing 13-per-cent current efficiency.

At very low temperatures, however, bright plating is impossible with a bath of this composition since chromic oxide or a similar compound is deposited along with the metal.

The Effect of Sulphate on the Quality of Chromium Deposited.

The ratio between the concentrations of chromic acid and sulphate can not be varied to a great extent without seriously affecting the behavior of the bath. In order to determine the limits of beneficial sulphate concentrations the following experiment was made in connection with the present research.

Five hundred cubic centimeters of a 250-gram-per-liter solution of chromic acid was placed in a steel tank connected anodically. Copper test strips used as cathodes were inserted in the bath and current was applied. When a low current density was used neither metal nor gas was deposited at the cathode. The current merely caused reduction of the hexavalent chromium in the bath to a lower valence. At a high current density, in addition to the reduction of hexavalent chromium, a copious evolution of hydrogen took place. Current densities up to 50 amperes per square decimeter at 25°C., approximately 470 amperes per square foot, caused no deposition of metal. At the higher current densities a stain was formed. This stain did not possess the luster of pure metal. In some cases copper was actually dissolved from the cathode as was shown by etching of the copper strip.

Upon adding small increments of sulphate, very little change in behavior was noted except that under certain conditions a greater amount of a brown film of a lower oxide or hydroxide of chromium was deposited at the cathode. At a sulphate concentration of 0.06 grams per liter, ratio $\frac{Cr^{VI}}{SO_4} = 2144$, there appeared specks of bright chromium scattered in a background of brown. Slightly more sulphate decreased the amount of adherent brown stain at the certain current densities. At 0.3 gram per liter of sulphate, ratio $\frac{Cr^{VI}}{SO_4} = 433$, bright plate was obtained on copper at 25°C. at 8 amperes per square decimeter. (74 amperes per square foot.) Increasing the current density caused the brown stain to reappear. At a sulphate concentration of 0.75 grams per liter $\frac{Cr^{VI}}{SO_4} = 173$, bright plate was obtained between 2.8–3.9 amperes per square decimeter (27 to 38 amperes per square foot) for a 120 second deposit.

As the sulphate concentration was increased still further the position and extent of the bright plating range was markedly influenced. Above a concentration of 6 grams per liter, ratio $\dfrac{Cr^{VI}}{SO_4} = 21.6$ of sulphate the bath behaved very unsatisfactorily. The cathode film was alternately formed and destroyed which resulted in violent fluctuations of current and potential, especially at current densities near the lower end of the plating range.

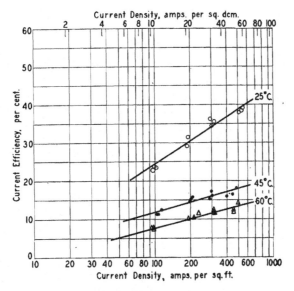

FIG. 3. Current Density-Current Efficiency Relationships. 235 g./l. CrO_3. $\dfrac{Cr^{VI}}{SO_4} = 102$.

Quantitative data are presented in Tables 7, 8, and 9 in Appendix A showing the effect of sulphate on the bright plating range on copper in a solution containing approximately 250 grams per liter of chromic acid. This work was done at 25°C., 45°C., and 60°C.

Although the results are necessarily rough due to the fact that personal judgment may differ in finding the point where a cathode just begins to show dull areas, yet the data are of sufficient accuracy to give an idea of the shifting of the bright plating range with changing sulphate concentrations and temperatures. These data will be referred to again and their usefulness made more apparent.

The Effect of Sulphate on the Yield of Metallic Chromium.

A quantitative study was then made to determine the effect of sulphate ion on the yield of chromium. The relationships of current density to current efficiency were determined at three temperatures on solutions containing various amounts of sulphate.

The baths contained 235 grams per liter of chromic acid and sufficient sulphate to make the ratio $\dfrac{Cr^{VI}}{SO_4}$ equal to 18.5, 46.3, 64.5, and 102.0 respec-

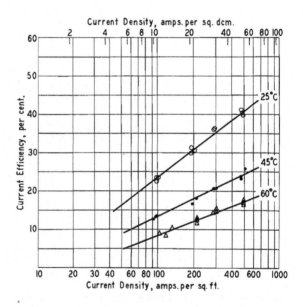

FIG. 4. Current Density-Current Efficiency Relationships. 235 g./l. CrO₃. $\dfrac{Cr^{VI}}{SO_4}$ = 64.5.

tively. Tests were made at 25°C., 45°C., and 60°C. and the current efficiencies were determined as before. At 60°C. a bath was also run whose $\dfrac{Cr^{VI}}{SO_4}$ ratio was 30. The results are given in the Appendix in Tables 10 to 22. These data are presented graphically in Figures 3, 4, 5 and 6 in which current efficiency is plotted as the ordinate and current density as the abscissa. Semi-logarithmic paper was used as in Figure 1. It is evident that for these solutions also a straight line relationship exists between current efficiency and the logarithm of the current density.

In order to give a comprehensive picture of the behavior of chromic-acid plating solutions, the results given in Tables 2, 3, 4 and 10 to 22 have been all combined and are presented in three master charts, Figures 7, 8, and 9.

The first chart, Figure 7, shows the behavior of a bath containing 230–235 grams per liter of chromic acid at 25°C. The ordinates are expressed in terms of both sulphate concentration and $\frac{Cr^{VI}}{SO_4}$ ratio. The abscissae are cathode current densities plotted on a logarithmic scale. In the body

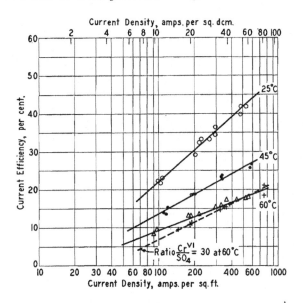

FIG. 5. Current Density-Current Efficiency Relationships. 235 g./l. CrO$_3$. $\frac{Cr^{VI}}{SO_4}$ = 46.3.

of the graph iso-current-efficiency lines are drawn in solid lines. The range of bright plate taken from Table 7 is marked in dotted lines. This bright plate range was worked out for deposits up to 0.0007 mm. (0.00003 in.) in thickness on copper cathodes. Optimum conditions for any metal for deposits of any thickness are always found very close to an iso-efficiency line representing 13-per-cent cathode current efficiency.

Figures 8 and 9 present the same information for solutions at 45°C. and 60°C., respectively.

It is to be noted that the bright range lines roughly parallel the cathode current efficiency lines except at low sulphate concentrations. At low sulphate concentrations there is a more copious evolution of hydrogen. Probably the rate of hydrogen deposition affects the cathode film unfavorably and the range of bright plate is thereby narrowed.

At high sulphate concentrations very unsatisfactory plating is obtained. From a study of the master charts a chromic acid to sulphate ratio, $\dfrac{Cr^{VI}}{SO_4}$, of between 40 to 60 would be recommended for solutions containing between 230 and 250 grams per liter of chromic acid.

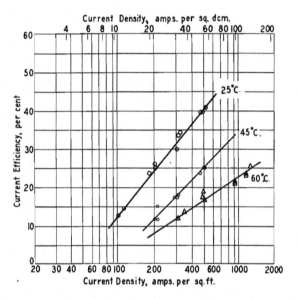

Fig. 6. Current Density-Current Efficiency Relationships. 235 g./l. CrO$_3$. $\dfrac{Cr^{VI}}{SO_4} = 18.5$.

The Effect of Chromic Acid Concentration on the Quality and Yield of Metallic Chromium.

At the present time there is no great uniformity of practice and opinion regarding the most propitious chromic acid concentration. Sargent worked with both saturated and comparatively dilute solutions with apparently little expressed preference for one or the other. His most satisfactory deposit was plated from a bath containing 25 per cent chromic acid and 0.3 per cent chromic sulphate, about 300 and 3 grams per liter respectively.

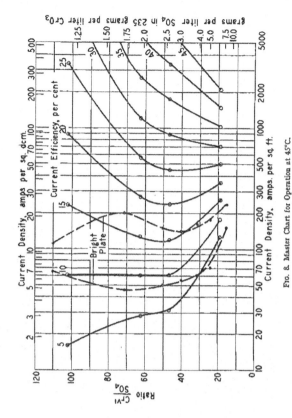

Fig. 8. Master Chart for Operation at 45°C.

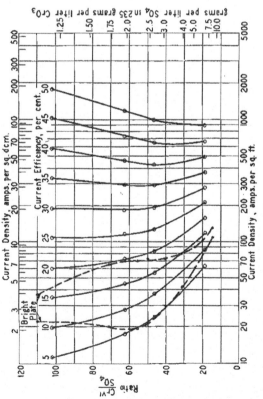

Fig. 7. Master Chart for Operation at 25°C.

These charts show the relationships between cathode current density, sulphate concentration of the bath, yield and nature of deposit at the temperatures 25°C., 45°C., and 60°C. (77°F., 113°F., and 140°F.) respectively. The baths contain 235 grams per liter of chromic acid. The bright plate range was determined for copper cathodes with deposits 0.0007 mm. (0.00003 in.) thick. Best plating conditions are found at 13 per cent cathode current efficiency. At $\frac{Cr^{VI}}{SO_4}$ ratios smaller than 25 or 20 the bath becomes commercially very unsatisfactory; a ratio near 50 is recommended.

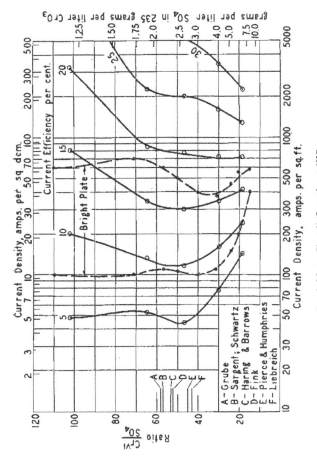

Fig. 9. Master Chart for Operation at 60°C.

Haring and Barrows favored a concentration of 250 grams per liter of chromic acid, as do many others. At present in the automobile industry 250 grams per liter or less is generally used while in many Eastern installations a concentration near 400 grams per liter is apparently favored.

According to Haring and Barrows "a decrease in the CrO_3 concentration is accompanied by a desirable increase in efficiency but also by an undesirable increase in resistivity; and conversely."

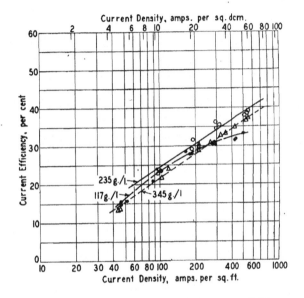

FIG. 10. Current Density-Current Efficiency Relationships. $\dfrac{Cr^{VI}}{SO_4} = 102$. Temperature 25°C. Note: straight-line relationship does not hold in the dilute solution.

It is presumable that a compromise is made at 250 grams per liter where slight changes in sulphate concentration do not affect the ratio, $\dfrac{Cr^{VI}}{SO_4}$, so markedly as at a lower chromic-acid concentration and where the spray and dragout losses are not so great as at higher chromic-acid concentrations.

A quantitative study was made by the present investigator in order to extend the work of Sargent and of Haring and Barrows on the effect of chromic-acid concentration. Solutions described in Tables 10 to 22 were diluted by adding an equal amount of water. Thus the $\dfrac{Cr^{VI}}{SO_4}$ ratios remained the same but the chromic-acid concentration was only 117 grams per liter. Measurements to determine the relation of current density to current efficiency were made at 25°C. and the bright range was determined. Similar tests were conducted on solutions whose $\frac{Cr^{VI}}{SO_4}$ ratios were the same as the above, but whose chromic-acid concentrations were 345 grams per liter. The results are given in Tables 23 to 30 in the Appendix and in Figures 10, 11, 12 and 13.

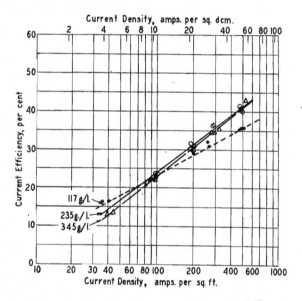

Fig. 11. Current Density-Current Efficiency Relationships. $\frac{Cr^{VI}}{SO_4} = 64.5$. Temperature 25°C.

Figure 10 shows the relationship between current density and current efficiency at 25°C. for a chromic-acid bath containing sufficient sulphate to make the ratio $\frac{Cr^{VI}}{SO_4}$ equal 102. The three lines show this condition for solutions containing 117, 235, and 345 grams per liter of chromic acid, respectively. It is interesting to note that for the dilute solution the straight-line relationship does not always hold. In Figures 11 and 12, the straight-line relationship does hold in the ranges of current density investigated for $\frac{Cr^{VI}}{SO_4}$ ratios of 64.5 and 46.3, respectively.

In general dilute solutions gas more strongly than do concentrated ones under the same conditions. Also the range of bright plate is appreciably narrowed. There is, however, no very marked difference in current efficiency except at isolated points. Usually any increase or decrease in efficiency accompanying dilution does not hold true over the entire range of current densities investigated.

In order to determine more carefully the effect of chromic-acid concentration on the quality of the deposit, the bright plating range was found for

TABLE 31

Bright Plating Range on Copper Cathodes at 25°C.

Ratio $\dfrac{Cr^{VI}}{SO_4} = 50$

Maximum thickness of deposit 0.0007 mm. (0.00003 in.)

CrO_3 concentration	LOWER LIMIT		UPPER LIMIT		EXTENT	
g./l.	amp./dcm².	amp./ft².	amp./dcm².	amp./ft².	amp./dcm².	amp./ft².
100	2.8	26	4.8	45	2.0	19
150	2.7	25	4.7	44	2.0	19
200	2.7	25	7.7	72	5.0	47
235	2.3	21	7.9	73	5.6	52
250	2.5	23	8.3	77	5.8	54
275	3.5	33	9.1	85	5.6	52
350	3.9	36	10.2	95	6.3	59
400	3.4	32	9.4	87	6.0	55
600			Very narrow limits			

a series of solutions of varying concentrations whose $\dfrac{Cr^{VI}}{SO_4}$ ratios were 50. The results are given in Table 31 and graphically in Figure 14.

In Figure 14 the abscissae are current densities and the ordinates represent the chromic-acid concentration. The limiting current densities between which bright plate is obtained on copper for a maximum thickness of 0.0007 mm. at 25°C. are drawn in. From these rather rough data the best chromic-acid concentration from the viewpoint of throwing power and bright plate range would be one in the vicinity of 350 grams per liter. At this concentration, however, spray and drag-out losses became more appreciable and in choosing a commercial bath all these factors must be considered. Dilutions under 150 grams per liter of chromic acid should be avoided not only because the plating range is narrowed but also because the fuming is greater than in a more concentrated solution and because according to Haring and Barrows[99] the resistance of the bath is increased somewhat.

[99] Bureau of Standards. Technologic Paper 346. Page 427.

The Effect of pH on the Yield of Metallic Chromium.

Haring and Barrows proved conclusively that ordinary "buffers" such as chromic hydroxide, chromic oxide, iron dichromate have no appreciable effect on the acidity of the bath. The pH of a 2.5M chromic-acid bath has been shown to be considerably below 1 and inasmuch as the concentration of chromic acid is so high, small increments of other materials can not materially change the acidity.

They determined the relationships between current density and current efficiency on baths made up of chromic acid to which had been added

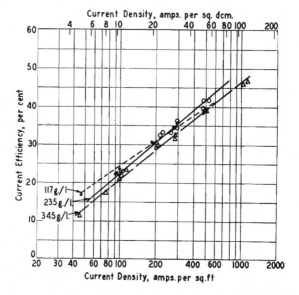

FIG. 12. Current Density-Current Efficiency Relationships. $\frac{Cr^{VI}}{SO_4} = 46.3$. Temperature 25°C.

equivalent amounts of sulphuric acid, chromium sulphate, and chromium sulphate and chromium carbonate, respectively. This was thought to give an acid, a neutral, and an alkaline bath. There was no measurable difference in their behavior.

Some of the present writer's early work was done with barium chromate as a buffer. This substance was used because it introduced no foreign anion, no appreciable amounts of cation, and no trivalent chromium. Results with this material were identical to those when barium chromate was not added.

The Effect of Trivalent Chromium and Iron on the Quality and Yield of Metallic Chromium.

All chromic acid plating baths in general use contain trivalent chromium, or iron, or both, either added intentionally or formed during electrolysis. The mechanism of this latter process will be taken up later. In order to study the effect of these two materials a bath was electrolyzed intermittently, at a low temperature, and with steel anodes, for 332 ampere hours.

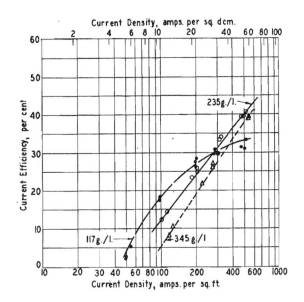

FIG. 13. Current Density-Current Efficiency Relationships. $\frac{Cr^{VI}}{SO_4} = 18.5$. Temperature 25°C. Note: straight-line relationship does not hold in the dilute solution.

These conditions as will be explained in detail later are conducive to the formation of trivalent chromium and to the solution of iron. The volume of the bath was 850 cubic centimeters.

The initial and final compositions of the bath were as follows:

	HEXAVALENT Cr	TRIVALENT Cr	TRIVALENT Fe	TOTAL TRIVALENT Fe + TRIVALENT Cr
	g./l.	g./l.	g./l.	g./l.
Initial	126.0	0	0	0
Final	111.2	17.0	5.3	22.3

A second bath, after 480 ampere hours operation, gave results comparable with the first.

	HEXAVALENT Cr	TRIVALENT Cr	TRIVALENT Fe	TOTAL TRIVALENT Fe + TRIVALENT Cr
	g./l.	g./l.	g./l.	g./l.
Initial	126.0	0	0	0
Final	105.0	18.0	4.9	22.9

A layer of kerosene on the surface of the bath prevented spray losses. Thus no sulphate was lost. Chromic acid was added from time to time to maintain a constant chromium content.

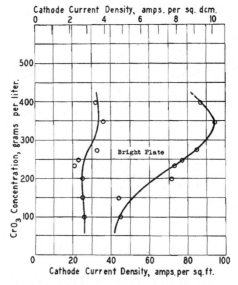

FIG. 14. Effect of CrO_3 Concentration on Quality of Plate. Temperature 25°C. $\frac{Cr^{VI}}{SO_4} = 50$. Copper cathodes. Thickness of deposit 0.0007 mm. (0.00003 in.).

The sulphate content was 2.52 g./l.; sufficient so that initially the ratio by weight of $Cr^{VI}/SO_4 = 50$.

The current density-current efficiency relationship was determined by depositing chromium from these two final baths, and from mixtures of these with unused baths, having the same Cr^{VI}/SO_4 ratio but containing no trivalent chromium and trivalent iron. The results are presented in Table 32.

TABLE 32

Effect of Foreign Element on Current Density-Current Efficiency Relationship

Temperature 25°C.

TRIVALENT CHROMIUM AND IRON		CATHODE CURRENT DENSITY		CURRENT EFFICIENCY	APPEARANCE
Cr	Fe				
g./l.	g./l.	amp./dcm^2.	amp./ft^2.	per cent	
0.0	0.0	5.8	53.5	13.9	3
		10.8	100.9	22.8	3+
		22.5	209.0	29.9	3+
		45.8	426.0	38.5	4
4.0	1.0	6.2	57.5	14.3	3
		11.1	103.7	22.0	3+
		45.0	418.0	38.6	4
8.0	2.0	9.4	87.8	20.5	3+
		21.6	201.0	32.3	3+
		39.8	370.0	36.5	4
12.0	3.0	5.4	50.2	13.9	3+
		10.9	101.2	20.7	3+
15.0	4.0	3.0	28.3	10.5	3
		4.7	43.5	12.9	3
		19.2	178.2	28.9	4
17.0	4.7	2.0	19.0	6.9	3
		2.5	23.1	7.4	3
		3.6	34.3	12.2	3+
		8.5	79.5	21.6	4
		28.7	267.0	32.0	4
		35.0	326.0	34.5	4

However, when the concentrations of trivalent chromium and iron were increased to 18.0 and 4.9 g./l., respectively, current efficiency measurements could not be obtained. This was due to the fact that the voltage and current pulsated violently.

These observations were confirmed by an examination of a commercial bath. This bath had been operated for a year with steel anodes for depositing a 90-second plate on bumper bars. The analysis indicated the presence of 150 g./l. of hexavalent chromium, 19.4 g./l. of trivalent chromium, 19.1 g./l. of Fe, and 4.98 g./l. of SO_4. At 45°C. no current efficiency measurements could be made, due to the fluctuating current. Electrolysis to obtain a bright plating range of current densities gave very inconsistent results.

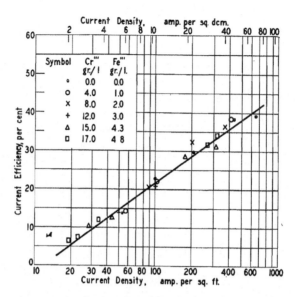

Fig. 15. Current Density-Current Efficiency Relationship at 25°C. of Chromium Plating Baths Containing Trivalent Chromium and Iron. Cr^{VI} 105 to 126 g./l. SO_4 2.52 g./l.

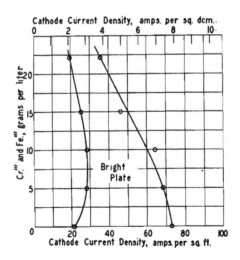

Fig. 16. Effect of Trivalent Chromium and Iron on Quality of Plate. $\dfrac{\overline{Cr^{VI}}}{SO_4} = 50$. Temperature 25°C. Copper Cathodes. Thickness of deposit 0.0007 mm. (0.00003 in.).

These data are all plotted on the same diagram in Fig. 15. It is apparent that only one line can be drawn through these points, and that within the limits reported trivalent chromium and trivalent iron do not affect the current density-current efficiency relationships of a bath.

In addition to the figures in Table 29, a large number of qualitative tests, with deposits of 0.0007 mm. (0.00003 in.) thickness, without current efficiency determinations, were made in order to find the limits of current density between which bright or "3" plates were produced. These results are presented in Table 33 and Figure 16. It is to be noted that the limits are contracted with increasing trivalent chromium and iron concentrations.

TABLE 33

Effect of Trivalent Chromium and Iron on Range of Cathode Current Densities Producing Good Plate

Temperature 25°C.

TRIVALENT CHROMIUM AND IRON			BRIGHT PLATING RANGE			
Cr	Fe	Total	Lower Limit		Upper Limit	
$g./l.$	$g./l.$	$g./l.$	$amp./dcm^2.$	$amp./ft^2.$	$amp./dcm^2.$	$amp./ft^2.$
0	0	0	2.2	21	7.8	73
4.0	1.0	5.0	3.0	28	7.3	68
8.0	2.0	10.0	3.0	28	7.0	65
12.0	3.0	15.0	2.7	25	4.8	45
17.0	4.7	22.2	2.0	19	3.8	35

The lower limit is about 10 per cent higher on the highly buffered side than on the smooth side. These figures are average. These results hold for copper cathodes and a deposit of 0.0007 mm. (0.00003 in.) thickness. Observation of the behavior of a bath containing 8 g./l. of trivalent chromium and 96 g./l. of trivalent iron would ascribe this effect to the chromium alone and not to the iron.

It was found that when a large amount of trivalent chromium was present in the bath, a brown stain deposited along with the metallic chromium. This film was more or less capable of being wiped off. Such a film is also produced when the sulphate content of a bath is too low, and when the temperature of plating is too low as has been pointed out before. It is not impossible that these factors affect in some related manner the type of ionization of the chromic acid.

The Effect of Other Addition Agents.

Trivalent chromium and iron are not always addition agents in the true sense of the word but in this bulletin the term addition agent will be used to cover all materials not essential to the process. Copper and calcium have been suggested. Hosdowich[h] advocated the use of any metallic ion lower than chromium in the electromotive series for the purpose of increasing throwing power. Wurker[i] and Long, Gardam, and MacNaughtan[j] also suggested a large number of metallic ions. None of these, however, in the amounts prescribed have been found in the present investigation to have any appreciable effect on the cathode.

Ewing and Malloy[87] made a study of additions of small quantities of substances such as mercury and of organic materials such as benzol. They showed that surface tensions were lowered and a colloid was formed. This resulted in a finer grained deposit.

The Effect of the Nature of Anodes on the Quality and Yield of Metallic Chromium.

Anodes of various materials have been used for plating from chromic-acid baths. Watts[100] reported different yields and types of deposit resulting from the use of different anode materials. In order to determine whether this effect was due to the anode materials or to the changes in bath composition arising from their use the following experiment was made in connection with the present research.

Copper strips were plated with a very thin layer of chromium from a chromic-acid bath. In one case lead anodes were inserted: in the others, anodes of iron, platinum, and graphite. No difference was observed in the behavior of the bath or in the quality of metal deposited.

A 25-hour run was made in which three solutions were electrolyzed in series in order to insure equal cathode current densities. Naturally the cathodes used had the same area. Steel, platinum, and lead respectively were used as anodes. Graphite was not used because it disintegrates rapidly in chromic acid solutions. The current efficiencies proved to be 12.9, 12.3, and 13.1 per cent, respectively. The deposits were quite similar; the plate obtained with lead anodes was the brightest. It is evident, therefore, that the effect of different anode materials is indirect. They cause changes in the bath composition which in turn affects the deposit.

[h] U. S. P. 1590170 (1926).
[i] Fr. P. 607829 (1926).
[j] Brit. P. 258724 (1926).
[87] Mich. State College Engineering Experiment Station Bulletin No. 7 (1926).
[100] Trans. Am. Electrochem. Soc. 52: 177–185 (1927).

Other Factors Affecting the Quality of Deposit.

As has been pointed out before, at 25°C. about ten per cent higher current density was required to reach the lower limit of the plating range on buffed copper than on copper having a smooth, rolled finish. In general, however, the rougher the surface, the greater is the current density required because a rough surface presents a greater area for plating than a smooth surface of the same dimensions.

The cathode material affects the nature of the deposit. For example, copper and brass can readily be plated with a bright deposit at room temperature; steel and nickel must be plated at above 35°C.; zinc cannot be plated with a bright deposit at any temperature. These statements hold for thin deposits. If a thick plate is made the under metal has less effect on the quality because for most of the plating time chromium has been depositing upon chromium.

A light film of oxide on copper also results in a dull plate.

In the foregoing sections of the bulletin the bright plate range has been described for thin deposits on copper. It is obvious that dull plate can be obtained within this range if cathode conditions are not right, for example, if a copper cathode is slightly oxidized, or if a steel cathode is plated at room temperature. Yet, under such conditions if a heavy plate is deposited, it may be bright due to the fact that the original cathode surface can only affect the nature of the first flash of plate. After that, metal is depositing upon chromium and a normal deposit can be expected.

SECTION II. THE EFFECTS OF BATH COMPOSITION, NATURE OF ANODES, AND PLATING CONDITIONS ON ANODE BEHAVIOR

It will be necessary to discuss briefly some phases of the mechanism of chromium deposition in order to understand more clearly the function of the anode. During plating the current supplied accomplishes several things.

At the Cathode.
1. Hydrogen is discharged and liberated.
2. Hexavalent chromium is reduced to the trivalent form.
3. Chromium is deposited.

The second process is undoubtedly quite a complex reaction in which probably some divalent ions are formed. These are then oxidized by the chromic acid to the more stable trivalent form.

At the Anode
1. Oxygen is liberated.
2. The anode is dissolved.
3. Trivalent chromium is oxidized back to the hexavalent form.

It is obvious that the extent of solution of the anode and of reoxidation of chromium will affect the composition of the solution. Solution composition, as has been demonstrated before, profoundly affects the reactions at the cathode. It has been possible, however, to measure cathode current efficiencies with respect to metal deposition and to observe the nature of the deposits as a problem quite distinct from anode reactions. This has been true because changes in solution composition, occurring in the short time necessary for these determinations, were negligible.

On the other hand it is obvious that the problems of oxidation and reduction of chromium and of the solution of the anode are so closely related that they are best treated together. For this reason in this section only a brief consideration will be given to some of the more general characteristics of anode behavior during chromium plating.

The Ideal Anode.

The ideal anode for chomic-acid baths would be one possessing the following properties:
1. Fair electrical conductivity.
2. An adherent oxide.
3. Fair electrical conductivity of the oxide.
4. Relatively low solubility of metal and oxide in chromic acid.
5. High oxygen overvoltage on both metal and oxide.

Some materials when used as anodes fail due to their anodic solubility in chromic acid. Watts made a rather complete investigation of the suitability of various metals and alloys and found that due to their anodic solubility, the plating baths soon became inoperable. He gives the following table to show the relative rates of solution of the different materials:

RATE OF SOLUTION OF ANODES IN CHROMIUM PLATING

ANODE	G./AMP. BR.
Chromium	0.371
Ferrochromium	0.324
Stainless steel	0.383
Steel	0.0084
Nickel	0.062
Nickel-silicon, 5 per cent	0.973
Nickel-chromium	0.663
Ferrochromium-silicon	0.740
Duriron	0.0135
Chromium deposited at cathode	0.0453 (14% efficiency)

Tantalum and its oxide are only very slightly soluble in chromic-acid baths. Yet tantalum fails as an anode because the oxide has so low an electrical conductivity that the necessary voltage soon grows to a prohibitive figure. Graphite has proved quite unsatisfactory because it disintegrates in the bath. Thus only iron, lead, and platinum remain as possible anode materials for these metals are soluble to so low an extent that they have been proved satisfactory from this standpoint.

The comparison of these metals may be made from another point of view. The rate at which trivalent chromium is reoxidized is intimately bound up with the magnitude of the oxygen overvoltage on the anode. In order to determine their relative capacities for reoxidizing trivalent chromium, the following experiment was made:

Three 150 cc. baths containing 234 g./l. of chromic acid and 4.42 g./l. of potassium sulphate were run in series. The anodes were of steel, lead, and platinum, respectively. After 25.5 hours' electrolysis at 35°C. with both anode and cathode current densities at 6.9 amp./sq. dm. (63.5 amp./sq. ft.), the trivalent chromium concentrations were determined. A record of results is given in Table 34.

TABLE 34
Electrolysis with Various Anodes

ANODE	INITIAL TRIVALENT Cr	FINAL TRIVALENT Cr	INITIAL VOLTAGE	FINAL VOLTAGE	CATHODE CURRENT EFFICIENCY
	g./l.	g./l.			per cent
Steel	0	3.74	3.22	3.81	12.9
Platinum	0	1.68	3.22	3.32	12.3
Lead	0	0.55	3.22	3.24	13.1

Since the cathodes were identical in size and composition it is to be expected that identical cathode reactions took place. The agreement in cathode current efficiencies of metal deposition bears out this view.

At the anode, naturally, similar but not identical reactions took place in each case. For example, some steel went into solution, for the bath gave a positive test for iron; some lead dissolved and formed a precipitate of lead chromate; only the platinum was not markedly affected. Oxygen was liberated at each anode but as it was not measured, no quantitative figures can be given. The abilities of these anodes to reoxidize trivalent chromium to the hexavalent form can be compared in Column 2, which presents the amount of trivalent chromium that they had failed to oxidize. It can be seen that lead, platinum, and iron are valuable in this order as anode material. This experiment was necessary because ordinary oxygen overvoltage values given in text books may not be a measure of the anode behavior of materials covered more or less completely with an oxide of indefinite composition.

Fig. 17

Since the cost of platinum is prohibitive, only steel and lead anodes will be given further consideration. Iron and steel have been found commercially satisfactory from all standpoints but that of solubility. Although iron is entirely passive in contact with chromic acid when no current is flowing, prolonged use as anodes will result in an accumulation of dissolved or colloidally suspended iron compounds in the bath.

Lead is more satisfactory than iron with respect to the oxygen overvoltage and its effect on the bath. This will be discussed in detail later. During electrolysis lead usually is less soluble than iron. Lead exhibits a tendency to become more soluble at high bath temperatures. The solubility of lead, however, fortunately does not present any real difficulties in practice because the lead ion immediately reacts with the bath forming a precipitate of lead chromate. This is harmful only when it forms as an adherent coating on the anode. Some grades of lead, however, have proved appreciably soluble in chromic acid when merely suspended therein. In the present investigation, after a period of three weeks' disuse, sheet-lead anodes $\frac{3}{8}$ inch thick were found pitted and corroded almost through.

The following photograph, Figure 17, shows the pitting which took place in the lead anode. The lead proved on analysis to contain 0.5 per cent of antimony.

SECTION III. THE EFFECTS OF BATH COMPOSITION, NATURE OF ANODES, AND PLATING CONDITIONS ON THE ULTIMATE OR EQUILIBRIUM BATH COMPOSITION

The presence of trivalent chromium in a chromic-acid plating bath has been shown by Haring and Barrows[99] to be detrimental. They explain this on the basis that trivalent chromium ions combine with chromic acid to form a colloidal chromium dichromate. In this manner there is less "free" chromic acid remaining to carry the current, and the resistance of the bath increases many fold. They stated that if lead anodes are used, the resulting concentration of trivalent chromium would not be harmful; if, however, steel anodes are used, it would lead to the formation of excessive amounts of this compound.

Results obtained in the laboratory, and in many commercial establishments, with the use of steel anodes have been such that it seemed questionable whether objectionable amounts of "chromium dichromate" are formed through their use. At any rate it was felt desirable not only to investigate the matter of the formation of trivalent chromium through the use of iron or steel anodes, but also to obtain a more or less quantitative comparison of iron and lead anodes from this standpoint.

[99] Loc. cit.

A Study of the Concentration of Trivalent Chromium at Equilibrium and of the Rate of Solution of Iron.

Five steel tanks of 500 cc. volume, functioning as anodes and connected in series were filled with chromic-acid plating solutions. A sixth tank was fitted up with lead anodes. These solutions differed from each other only in their trivalent chromium concentrations. Metallic chromium was deposited from these baths on steel cathodes for from 90 to 138 hours. The hexavalent chromium concentration, temperature and current density were kept as constant as possible. At various intervals of time, samples were taken from the baths for analysis.

Tanks made of 0.09 per cent carbon steel holding the plating baths functioned also as anodes. They were about 7.6 cm. (3 in.) in diameter and 17.8 cm. (7 in.) tall. The lead anodes used were about 2.5 cm. (1 in.) wide and 17.8 cm. (7 in.) long, only a portion of which extended into the bath. The area of the iron anodes was approximately 3.4 sq. dm. (0.3565 sq. ft.); that of the lead anodes 0.59 sq. dm. (0.063 sq. ft.).

The cathodes also were of steel, having an area of 0.52 sq. dm. (0.0445 sq. ft.).

The six cells were connected in series, and 9.5 amperes were passed through. Hence the anode current densities lay between 2.7 and 2.9 amp./sq. dm. (25 and 27 amp./sq. ft.) for the steel anodes and about 16.2 amp./sq. dm. (150 amp./sq. ft.) for the lead anodes. The cathode current densities were 21.6 amp./sq. dm. (200 amp./sq. ft.).

The tanks were placed side by side in the constant-temperature tank filled with kerosene. By means of a steam and cold water coil in the kerosene, the temperature of the baths was maintained close to 45°C.

Five of the baths were prepared by mixing a solution containing 234 g./l. of chromic acid with sufficient potassium sulphate (4.42 g./l.) so that the weight ratio of hexavalent chromium to sulphate, Cr^{VI}/SO_4, was 50.

"Chemically pure" chromium hydroxide made by the J. T. Baker Company was added in varying amounts in order to furnish trivalent chromium. It is interesting to note that about half of the amount added actually dissolved, the rest remained as an inert sludge. The hydroxide contained 5.77 per cent of sulphate as an impurity. As a part of this was soluble, this addition must have decreased slightly the ratio Cr^{VI}/SO_4.

Another bath, prepared according to the specifications of Grube[48] contained 234 g./l. of chromic acid, 3 g./l. of chromium sulphate and 6 g./l.

[48] U. S. P. 1496845 (1924).

A STUDY OF CHROMIUM PLATING

of chromium hydroxide. Table 35 shows the proportions of materials used in the preparation of the baths in grams per liter.

Thirty-six hours were allowed for digesting before the solutions were analyzed for trivalent chromium. Then the solutions were electrolyzed. At various intervals during electrolysis the solutions were sampled and analyzed for trivalent chromium. Water and chromic acid were added from time to time to maintain the volume and chromium content of the

TABLE 35
Composition of Baths as Made Up in Grams per Liter

	CrO_3	$Cr(OH)_3$	K_2SO_4	$Cr_2(SO_4)_3$	ANODE
1	234	2	4.42		Fe
2	234	20	4.42		Fe
3	234	50	4.42		Fe
4	234	100	4.42		Fe
5	234	6		3.0	Fe
6	234	0	4.42		Pb

TABLE 36
Trivalent Chromium Content of Baths during Electrolysis

TIME	AMPERE HOURS	TEMPERATURE	TRIVALENT CHROMIUM CONTENT OF TANKS					
			1	2	3	4	5	6
hours		°C.	g./l.	g./l.	g./l.	g./l.	g./l.	g./l.
0	0	45	0.8	7.1	13.9	22.5	2.5	0
6	54	45	3.4	7.2	11.8	20.0	5.2	
12	108	45	4.8	9.6	11.6	15.8	6.5	
34	306	45			7.6	12.2	9.0	1.4
66	594	45	9.6	11.0			8.2	
90	810	45	7.1	7.9	7.4	10.5	8.5*	
114	1,026	50	9.6					
138	1,242	50	8.8	9.7	9.9			1.5

* Anode current density higher than before.

baths. After 66 hours the chromium hydroxide sludge, which had lain as an inert mass at the bottom of the tanks, was filtered out and the electrolyses were continued. Little change in the composition of the solutions was noted as a result of filtration.

Table 36 shows the amounts of trivalent chromium in solution in the different baths at various stages of the electrolysis. The volume of each bath was 500 cc. These analyses are not so accurate as those in the remaining sections of the paper, due to the fact that different methods were

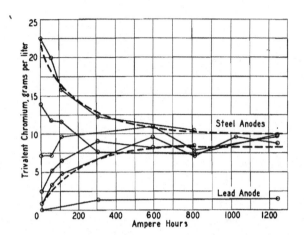

FIG. 18. Equilibrium Concentration of Trivalent Chromium at 45°C. Cathode current densities, 21.6 amp./sq. dm. (200 amp./sq. ft.); anode current densities, 2.7 to 2.9 amp./sq. dm. (25 to 27 amp./sq. ft.); cathodes, steel; volumes, 500 cc. 235 g/l. CrO_3 and 4.42 g./l. K_2SO_4. It can readily be seen that the concentration of trivalent chromium comes to equilibrium, a condition of steady state.

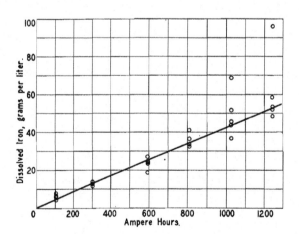

FIG. 19. Rate of Anodic Solution of Iron at 45°C. Cathode current densities, 21.6 amp./sq. dm. (200 amp./sq. ft.); anode current densities, 2.7 to 2.9 amp./sq. dm. (25 to 27 amp./sq. ft.); cathodes, steel; anodes, steel containing 0.09 per cent carbon; volumes, 500 cc. 235 g./l. CrO_3, 4.42 g./l. K_2SO_4.

being used while developing the procedure described on page 66. The results of the analyses are presented graphically in Fig. 18.

Where steel anodes were used, it was found that iron went into solution. In order to determine the rate of solution, analyses were made for iron in the solutions described above. The results are recorded in Table 37. No explanation can be given for the abnormal rate of solution of iron in tank No. 5. These results are shown graphically in Fig. 19.

The results of the study show that in a bath operating under fixed plating conditions and fairly constant chromic acid concentration the trivalent chromium concentration normally approaches an "equilibrium concentration," a condition of steady state.

Six solutions, differing only in their trivalent chromium concentrations, were run under identical plating conditions. The only additions made

TABLE 37
Iron Content of Baths during Electrolysis

TIME	AMPERE HOURS	TEMPERA- TURE	IRON CONTENT OF TANKS				
			1	2	3	4	5
hours		°C.	g./l.	g./l.	g./l.	g./l.	g./l.
0	0	45	0	0	0	0	0
12	108	45	5.1	5.2	7.6	4.0	6.0
34	306	45	11.2	12.5	12.4	13.4	13.3
66	594	45	18.5	24.1	23.7	27.0	24.6
90	810	45		41.2	32.6	33.4	36.3
114	1,026	50	43.4	45.4	51.6	36.8	68.7
138	1,242	50	58.8	52.1	53.6	48.5	96.2

were chromic acid and water. In five of these where steel anodes were used, in 90 hours, the trivalent chromium concentrations, which were initially between 0.8 and 22.5 g./l., gradually assumed values of from 7.1 to 10.5 g./l. Three of these were permitted to run an additional 48 hours, and their final trivalent chromium concentrations varied from 8.8 to 9.9 g./l.

Lead anodes in a bath operated under these conditions produced an equilibrium concentration of around 1.5 g./l. of trivalent chromium. Iron goes into solution at a constant rate, and will build up a concentration of dissolved iron indefinitely. From a consideration of these points, lead seems to be much superior to iron as an anode material.

TABLE 38
The Behavior of Chromium Plating Baths under the Influence of Steel and Lead Anodes
Temperature 65°C.

ANODE	ANODE CURRENT DENSITY		TIME	AMPERE HOURS	HEXA-VALENT Cr	TRIVA-LENT Cr	Fe	WEIGHT OF ANODE	LOSS IN WEIGHT
	amp./ft².	amp./dcm²	hours		g./l.	g./l.	g.		
Fe	20	2.2	0	0	126.0	0	0		
	20	2.2	38	247	128.5	8.0	12.7	*	
	20	2.2	72	468	131.7	†	21.9		
Fe	35	3.8	0	0	126.0	0	0	218.0	
	35	3.8	38	247	121.8	8.6	6.4		
	35	3.8	72	468	124.5	12.3	7.7	210.4	7.6
Fe	50	5.4	0	0	126.0	0	0	156.7	
	50	5.4	38	247	117.5	12.1	5.1		
	50	5.4	72	468	130.0	15.4	9.7	149.7	7.0
Pb	50	5.4	0	0	126.0	4.8	0	424.0	
	50	5.4	38	247	123.5	0.6	0		
	50	5.4	72	468	127.0	0.7	0	414.1	9.9‡

* No weights of anodes could be recorded because tanks were used as anodes.
† An accident destroyed this result.
‡ Waterline corrosion very marked.

TABLE 39
The Behavior of Chromium Plating Baths under the Influence of Steel Anodes
Temperature 60°C.

ANODE	ANODE CURRENT DENSITY		TIME	AMPERE HOURS	HEXA-VALENT Cr	TRIVA-LENT Cr	Fe	WEIGHT OF ANODE	LOSS IN WEIGHT
	amp./ft².	amp./dcm².	hours		g./l.	g./l.	g.		
Fe	20	2.2	0	0	126.0	0	0		
	20	2.2	36	234		4.6	14.9	*	
	20	2.2	72	468		4.3	27.6		
	20	2.2	100	650	125.0	3.4	34.1		
Fe	35	3.8	0	0	126.0	0	0	210.3	
	35	3.8	36	234	117.5	7.2	6.1		
	35	3.8	72	468		10.6			
	35	3.8	100	650	113.0	10.3	11.3	200.1	10.2
Fe	50	5.4	0	0	126.0	0	0	149.6	
	50	5.4	36	234	117.5	7.7	5.1		
	50	5.4	72	468		11.0	9.2		
	50	5.4	100	650	115.0	10.8	13.7	138.7	10.9
Fe	100	10.8	0	0	126.0	0	0	64.2	
	100	10.8	36	234	118.9	10.0	5.1		
	100	10.8	72	468		16.4	9.3		
	100	10.8	100	650	107.3	15.4	11.7	54.2	10.0

* Steel tank was used, hence weight could not be taken.

The Effect of Anode Current Density.

Where steel anodes are used successfully in practice usually the steel tank itself is connected anodically. Thus the anode area is quite large in comparison to the cathode area, and the anode current density will be low. There are cases, as in plating the inner surfaces of tubes, where a large anode area can not be provided. The purpose of this study was to determine whether the anode current density materially affected the equilibrium concentration of trivalent chromium and the rate of solution of iron.

The solution studied contained 234 g./l. of chromic acid. This was sufficient to make the weight ratio of hexavalent chromium to sulphate ion, Cr^{VI}/SO_4, equal to 50 as before.

Sets of six cells connected in series each contained the above solution, and were maintained under like conditions of current and temperature. They differed only in the size of the anodes used. In all cases except one the anodes were in two pieces, placed on opposite sides of a tall form 1,000 cc. beaker. In one case a very low anode current density was desired, and so a steel tank was used.

Additions of water or chromic acid or both were made from time to time in order to compensate for evaporation, for water decomposed by electrolysis, and for the amount of metal deposited. This procedure simulated actual plant practice.

Samples were taken at various intervals during electrolysis and analyzed in order to watch changes taking place in the bath. The analytical results reported in this section of the paper and in the sections following are satisfactorily accurate because the technique of the methods had been worked out. To insure additional accuracy, the fume and spray losses were avoided by the use of kerosene on the baths.

Test runs were made at 65°, 60°, and at 37°C. The data that are common to the three tests are as follows:

Cathode............ Steel
Cathode current density............... 14.8 amp./sq. dm. (137 amp./sq. ft.)
Initial bath composition............... Cr^r, 126 g./l.; SO_4, 2.52 g./l.
Current............. 6.5 amperes
Anodes............. Sheet steel, 0.13% carbon, and tube steel, 0.09% carbon
Volume of bath...... 850 cc. (steel tank 600 cc.)

The results of analyses taken during electrolyses are given in Tables 38, 39, and 40. All the analyses are reported in grams per liter except in the case of iron. Iron is reported in total grams in solution and was calculated by multiplying the concentration in grams per liter found by analyses by 0.85, the volume being 850 cc.

After the work represented by Table 38 was completed, it was found that the results told an incomplete story. An accident prevented further work on this set of solutions. The work shown in Table 39 was done at a slightly lower temperature. The volume of the bath in the case of steel tank anodes was 600 cc. Some of these results are also presented graphically in Figs. 20, 21, 22 and 23.

TABLE 40

The Behavior of Chromium Plating Baths under the Influence of Steel and Lead Anodes
Temperature 37°C.

ANODE	ANODE CURRENT DENSITY		TIME	AMPERE HOURS	HEXA-VALENT Cr	TRIVA-LENT Cr	Fe	WEIGHT OF ANODE	LOSS IN WEIGHT
	amp./ft.²	amp./dcm².	hours		g./l.	g./l.	g.		
Fe	35	3.8	0	0	125.0	0	0	222.7	
	35	3.8	39	253.5	121.5	5.8	3.5		
	35	3.8	72	468	117.9	6.3	4.7	218.0	4.7
Fe	50	5.4	0	0	125.0	0	0	141.6	
	50	5.4	39	253.5	126.5	7.8	3.7		
	50	5.4	72	468	114.0	8.9	4.5	136.5	5.1
Fe	100	10.8	0	0	125.0	0	0	68.2	
	100	10.8	39	253.5	126.5	7.6			
	100	10.8	72	468	111.8	9.3	4.2	64.2	4.0*
Fe	165	17.8	0	0	125.0	0	0	48.8	
	165	17.8	39	253.5	123.0	8.4	3.9		
	165	17.8	72	468	116.8	9.4	4.9	44.3	4.5
Pb	50	5.4	0	0	125.0	0	0	426.6	
	50	5.4	39	253.5	130.0	Trace	0		
	50	5.4	72	468	121.9	Trace	0	424.9	1.7
Pb	100	10.8	0	0	125.0	0	0	210.9	
	100	10.8	39	253.5	132.5	Trace	0		
	100	10.8	72	468	125.5	Trace	0	209.0	1.9

* Sludge was formed.

In Figs. 20 and 22, ampere hours of electrolysis are plotted against the concentration of trivalent chromium resulting. Figs. 21 and 23 show similarly the change in iron concentration in the baths. It is more accurate to use the figures given for dissolved iron found in the bath than those for loss in weight of the anodes. In Fig. 24, the equilibrium trivalent chromium concentration is plotted against anode current density. The equilibrium concentrations have been taken from the graphical data in Figs. 20 and 22, and can be summarized in Table 41.

Fig. 25 presents the result of plating at different anode current densities. It shows that anode current density has little, if any, effect upon the cathode

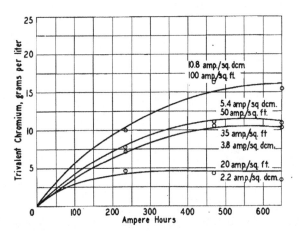

FIG. 20. Formation of Trivalent Chromium at 60°C. at Various Anode Current Densities. Cathode current densities, 14.8 amp./sq. dm. (137 amp./sq. ft.); cathodes and anodes, steel; initial bath composition, 234 g./l. CrO_3 + 4.56 g./l. K_2SO_4; volume of baths, 850 cc. (tank, 600 cc.).

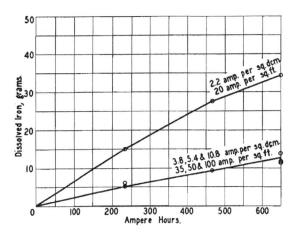

FIG. 21. Rate of Anodic Solution of Iron at 60°C. Cathode current densities, 14.8 amp./sq. dm. (137 amp./sq. ft.); cathodes and anodes, steel; initial bath composition, 234 g./l. CrO_3 + 4.56 g./l. K_2SO_4; volume of baths, 850 cc. (tank, 600 cc.).

deposit. The only possible effect it can have is in its effect upon solution composition, and this in turn can affect the plate. The specimens were

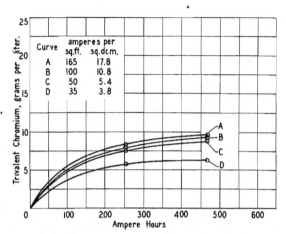

FIG. 22. Formation of Trivalent Chromium at 37°C. at Various Anode Current Densities. Cathode current densities, 14.8 amp./sq. dm. (137 amp./sq. ft.); cathodes and anodes, steel; initial bath composition, 234 g./l. CrO_3 + 4.56 g./l. K_2SO_4; volume of baths, 850 cc. (tank, 600 cc.).

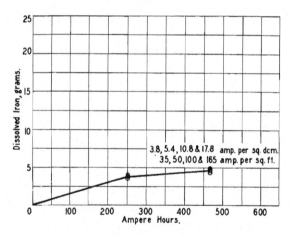

FIG. 23. Rate of Anodic Solution of Iron at 37°C. Cathode current densities, 14.8 amp./sq. dm. (137 amp./sq. ft.); cathodes and anodes, steel; initial bath composition, 234 g./l. CrO_3 + 4.56 g./l. K_2SO_4; volume of baths, 850 cc. (tank, 600 cc.).

plated at 60°C. with anode current densities, respectively, 10.8, 5.4, 3.8, and 2.2 amp./sq. dm. (100, 50, 35, and 20 amp./sq. ft.). The cathode current densities all were 14.8 amp./sq. dm. (137 amp./sq. ft.).

The solution in which the last specimen was plated contained a final iron

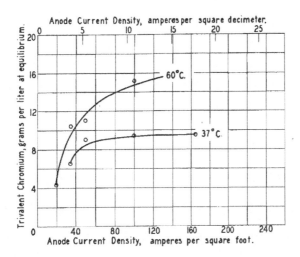

FIG. 24. Effect of Anode Current Density on Equilibrium Concentration of Trivalent Chromium. Anodes and cathodes, steel; initial bath composition, 243 g./l. CrO_3 + 4.56 g./l. K_2SO_4.

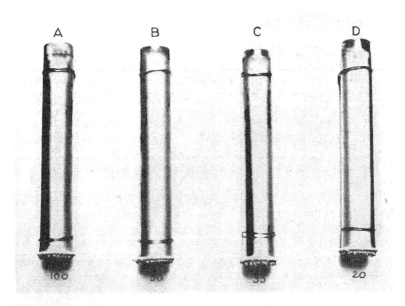

FIG. 25. Effect of Plating at Different Anode Current Densities. Anode current densities, 10.8, 5.4, 3.8 and 2.2 amp./sq. dm., respectively, from left to right. (100, 50, 35 and 20 amp./sq. ft.); cathode current densities, 14.8 amp./sq. dm. (137 amp./sq. ft.); initial bath composition, 243 g./l. CrO_3 + 4.42 g./l. K_2SO_4; temperature, 60°C. Note that anode current density has no effect on deposit.

concentration of about 50 g./l. The resulting plate contained 0.5 per cent of iron. When the samples were freshly plated no difference could be noted; upon standing several weeks the one containing 0.5 per cent iron became very slightly darker in color. It is believed that the iron was in portions of the solution entrapped in the voids in the chromium deposit rather than that it alloyed with the chromium.

TABLE 41

RELATIONSHIP BETWEEN ANODE CURRENT DENSITY AND TRIVALENT CHROMIUM CONTENT AT EQUILIBRIUM (STEEL ANODES)

ANODE CURRENT DENSITY		TEMPERATURE	EQUILIBRIUM TRIVALENT Cr CONCENTRATION
$amp./ft^2$.	$amp./dcm^2$.	°C.	g./l.
20	2.2	60	4.3
35	3.8	60	10.4
50	5.4	60	11.0
100	10.8	60	15.2
35	3.8	37	6.5
50	5.4	37	9.0
100	10.8	37	9.4
165	17.8	37	9.5

TABLE 42

THE EFFECT OF TEMPERATURE ON THE EQUILIBRIUM TRIVALENT CHROMIUM CONCENTRATION AND ON THE RATE OF SOLUTION OF IRON.

Solution $\dfrac{Cr^{VI}}{SO_4}$ = 50; Anodes, Steel; Anode c.d., 3.8 amp./sq.dm. (35 amp./ft.^{2}).

TEMPERATURE	TRIVALENT Cr	IRON DISSOLVED IN 468 AMP. HR.
°C.	g./l.	g.
37	6.5	4.5
45	8.5*	9.5*
60	10.5	9.2
65	12.5	9.7

* Not exactly comparable. Anode c. d. 2.8 to 3.2 amp./dcm.^{2} (25 to 30 amp./ft.^{2}).

The experimental work tends to show that the anode current density plays quite a definite part in determining the equilibrium trivalent chromium concentration. This conclusion is quite consistent with theory, because according to Le Blanc[k] and to Haring and Barrows[99] the capacity of an anode for oxidizing chromium to the hexavalent form is a function of the oxygen overvoltage on that metal or its oxide. The oxygen overvoltage is affected by anode current density, and varies according to a logarithmic

[k] Zeit. f. Elektrochemie 7, 291 (1900).
[99] Loc. cit.

equation. Müller and Soller,[1] however, believe that the capacity of an anode for oxidizing chromium to the hexavalent state is dependent upon the catalytic influence of the oxide formed on the anode surface which may be another way of saying the same thing.

The rate of solution of iron seems to be very slightly affected by anode area in the range studied; if anything, iron goes into solution somewhat more rapidly at low current densities than at high.

It would seem that in designing a chromium-plating equipment, it is wise to have such anode area that the average anode current density would be about 2.7 to 5.4 amp./sq. dm. (25 to 50 amp./sq. ft.). Higher anode current density leads to a greater equilibrium chromium concentration; lower current density to a more rapid rate of solution of iron.

Effect of Temperature.

The results just presented also indicate the part that temperature plays in determining the equilibrium concentration of trivalent chromium and the rate of solution of iron.

By examining the data in the tables and figures, it can be seen that the equilibrium trivalent chromium concentration increases with increasing temperature in approximately the manner recorded in Table 42.

Effect of Sulphate.

It was considered interesting to determine the effect of sulphate upon the equilibrium trivalent chromium concentration and upon the rate of solution of iron.

Several cells were run at 60°C. in which the anode current density was 5.4 amp./sq. dm. (50 amp./sq. ft.) and the solutions differed in sulphate concentration. The results of analyses of these baths during the period of electrolysis are given in Table 43.

It is apparent from these figures that the equilibrium trivalent chromium concentration and rate of solution of iron increase with the amount of sulphate present. The relationship in each case is almost a straight line relationship.

Fig. 26 shows the effect of sulphate upon the deposit. The specimen on the right was plated from a solution containing a deficiency of sulphate; that on the left from too much sulphate. The middle sample was plated from a correct bath.

[1] Zeit. f. Elektrochem. 11: 863 (1905).

The Results of Intermittent Electrolysis.

All of the work done up to this point represents continuous electrolyses, and in actual practice corresponds to the deposition of heavy, wear-resist-

TABLE 43

THE EFFECT OF SO_4 ON THE EQUILIBRIUM TRIVALENT CHROMIUM CONCENTRATION, AND ON THE RATE OF SOLUTION OF IRON

Cathode current density, 14.8 amp./dcm.^{2} (137 amp./ft.^{2}).

CONCEN-TRATION OF SO_4	RATIO $\dfrac{Cr^{VI}}{SO_4}$	TIME	AMPERE HOURS	HEXA-VALENT Cr	TRIVA-LENT Cr	Fe	WEIGHT OF ANODES	LOSS IN WEIGHT
g./l.		hours		g./l.	g./l.	g.	g.	
6.3	20	0	0	126.0	0	0	139.6	
6.3	20	36	234	105.2	22.4	5.2		
6.3	20	72	468		25.7	12.5		
6.3	20	100	650	101.9	23.6	7.9	131.8	7.8*
2.52	50	0	0	126.0	0	0	149.6	
2.52	50	36	234	117.5	5.1	5.1		
2.52	50	72	468		11.0	9.2		
2.52	50	100	650	115.0	10.8	13.7	138.7	10.9
1.26	100	0	0	126.0	0	0	130.3	
1.26	100	36	234	133.9	2.7	4.3		
1.26	100	72	468		2.5	8.6		
1.26	100	100	650	138.5	2.6	11.4	119.1	11.2

* Sludge formed.

TABLE 44

THE EFFECT OF DISCONTINUOUS PLATING ON THE EQUILIBRIUM TRIVALENT CHROMIUM CONCENTRATION AND ON THE RATE OF SOLUTION OF IRON.

Cathode Current Density, 14.8 amp./dcm.^{2} (137 amp./ft.^{2}).
Anode current density, 5.4 amp./sq. dm. (50 amp./sq. ft.)

TIME	PLATING TIME	AMPERE HOURS	HEXAVALENT Cr	TRIVALENT Cr	Fe	WEIGHT OF ANODES	LOSS IN WEIGHT
			Discontinuous plating				
hours	hours		g./l.	g./l.	g	g.	g.
0	0	0	126.0	0	0	138.7	
56	39.6	257.5	110.0	15.0	4.0		
72	51.0	332	111.2	17.0	4.5	134.5	4.2
104	73.8	480		18.0	4.1		
		Continuous plating under identical conditions. From Table 40					
0	0	0	125.0	0	0	141.6	
39	39	253.5	126.5	7.8	3.7		
72	72	468.0	114.0	8.9	4.5	136.5	5.1

ing plate. Many installations are for the purpose of depositing a light plate for decorative purposes. In this case work is constantly placed in and removed from the tank; current is alternately being applied and turned off.

In order to determine the effect of intermittent plating, an apparatus was devised to interrupt the current periodically and the electrolyte was analyzed from time to time. A commutator was driven by an electric

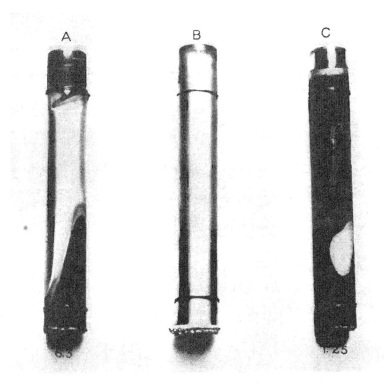

FIG. 26. Effect of Varying the Sulfate Content of Bath. Anode current density, 5.4 amp./sq. dm. (50 amp./sq. ft.); cathode current density, 14.8 amp./sq. dm. (137 amp./sq. ft.); anode and cathode, steel; bath composition, 243 g./l. $CrO_3 + SO_4$—6.3 g./l. in "A," 2.52 g./l. in "B," 1.26 g./l. in "C;" temperature, 60°C. Too much or too little sulphate produces poor plate.

motor through a system of reducing gears. In this manner a period of 23 seconds of plating and 3 seconds of nonplating was obtained.

A solution containing 243 g./l. of chromic acid and 4.56 g./l. of potassium sulphate was electrolyzed with lead anodes at 40°C. The anode current density was 5.3 amp./sq. dm. (50 amp./sq. ft.) the cathode current density was 13.5 amp./sq. dm. (125 amp./sq. ft.); the total current was 6.5 amperes. At the end of 48 hours, 42.5 hours of actual electrolysis, the trivalent chromium concentration had risen from 0 to 0.44 g./l.

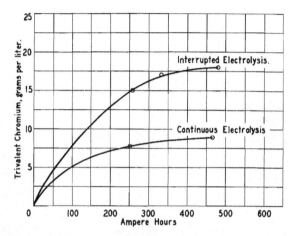

FIG. 27. Results of Interrupted Electrolysis on Trivalent Chromium Concentration. 37°C. Anode current density, 5.4 amp./sq. dm. (50 amp./sq. ft.); cathode current density, 14.8 amp./sq. dm. (137 amp./sq. ft.); anode and cathode, steel; initial bath composition, 243, g./l. CrO_3 + 4.56 g./l. K_2SO_4.

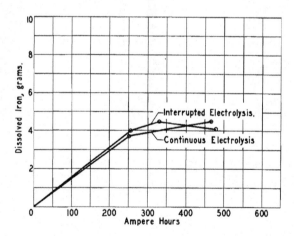

FIG. 28. Results of Interrupted Electrolysis on Rate of Anodic Solution of Iron. 37°C. 5.4 amp. per sq. dcm. (50 amp./sq. ft.) anode current density. Specifications as in Figure 27.

A greater amount of anode sludge, probably $PbCrO_4$, was formed than during a continuous electrolysis of similar length. The anode skin was very thin and chocolate colored, in contrast with a heavy, red coating formed by continuous electrolysis. The red coating on being scratched showed yellow lead chromate.

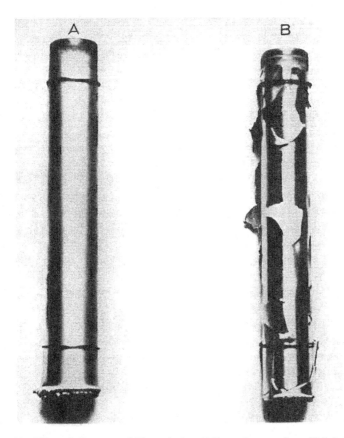

FIG. 29. Effect of Interrupted Electrolysis. "a" continuous plate, "b" interrupted plate—dull patches where plate flaked off. Anode current densities, 5.4 amp./sq. dm. (50 amp./sq. ft.); cathode current densities, 14.8 amp./sq. dm. (137 amp./sq. ft.); anodes and cathodes, steel; initial bath composition, 243 g./l. CrO_3 + 4.56 g./l. K_2SO_4; temperature, 37°C.

It was noted that in the three seconds with no current the voltage had not sufficient time to drop to the back e.m.f. of chromium in chromic acid. Therefore, the electrolysis was repeated with a period of 150 seconds on and 15 seconds off. After 16 hours (14.5 hours of actual plating) the trivalent chromium was very low, a few tenths of a gram per liter. This time the anode weights were recorded, and it was found that during this interval 1.8 grams of lead had been dissolved. In Table 40 it is shown that about 1.8 grams of lead dissolved in 72 hours, 468 ampere-hours, of continuous plating under otherwise identical conditions.

This electrolysis was repeated for a third time with steel anodes. The plating period was 110 seconds on and 45 seconds off. Analyses and current efficiency measurements were taken at the end of 56 and 72 hours. The results are presented in Table 44 and in Figs. 27 and 28. In order to check this point, the last electrolysis was duplicated for 104 hours, and the results are presented in the same table and figures.

The cathode in all these runs of intermittent plating was covered with badly cracked, peeling deposit. This deposit can readily be compared in Fig. 29 with a cathode plated under identical conditions except that electrolysis was continuous.

Tests were made on this solution after having been electrolyzed 0, 56, 72, and 104 hours, respectively, to determine what sort of results could be expected from baths of such compositions. It was found that although the current efficiencies were not noticeably changed, the range of current densities at which good plate can be obtained was contracted with increasing trivalent chromium and trivalent iron. This information has been fully dealt with in a previous section of this bulletin.

Intermittent plating favors the formation of a larger equilibrium trivalent chromium concentration than continuous plating produces. It does not affect the rate of iron solution materially.

If lead anodes are used, the oxygen overvoltage is so high that even intermittent electrolysis hardly affects the trivalent chromium concentration. The rate of corrosion of lead appears to be less during a period of continuous plating.

The presence of a foreign cation, such as iron or trivalent chromium, does not change the characteristics of the bath with respect to the current efficiencies obtained through its use. It does, however, contract the range of current densities producing good plate. It also increases the resistivity of the bath.

SECTION IV. MISCELLANEOUS NOTES ON CONTROL OF PLATING AND ON NATURE OF DEPOSITS

In the foregoing sections of this discussion it has been shown that changes in plating conditions, in bath compositions, seemingly of a trifling nature, can profoundly alter the nature of the results. A current density capable of producing bright plate at one temperature may be insufficient at a temperature 10°C. higher to produce any plate whatsoever. A change in sulphate concentration amounting to 0.2 per cent (2 grams per liter) can completely ruin a bath which had previously been operating satisfactorily.

Conditions such as these all require workable means for their control. There is still a great deal to be done before satisfactory control methods have been evolved. However, good practice of today has standardized some procedures which have met with sufficient success to recommend them.

Temperature is usually regulated by the use of two systems of lead or steel coils; one for cold water, the other for steam. The water coil is used infrequently because in general there is sufficient cooling due to evaporation and conduction so that heat usually needs to be added. In some installations steam and water are supplied to the same coil as needed by means of a suitable connection. In others the engineers have provided a system of two tanks; an inner one being separated from the outer by a space of several inches. Water or other suitable medium is kept in this space and is heated or cooled by coils. This procedure avoids the difficulties often encountered in finding materials for coils which will satisfactorily withstand chromic acid. Thermocouples or thermometers inserted in the tank operate a thermostat which regulates the steam input. Refined practice also calls for automatic temperature controlling and recording devices. In Europe, plating is very often done at room temperature or lower. In this case the steam coil is unnecessary and regulation is accomplished by proper manipulation of the cold water line. This practice, to be sure, often results in dull plate. Since, however, the current efficiency is greater than when bright plate is produced, and since labor for buffing is cheap, it is claimed to be economical both in England and on the Continent to plate in a cold tank.

Control of current density does not usually offer any great difficulty to the plater. With a given solution, in a tank where anode to cathode distances are fixed, it has been found fairly satisfactory to plate roughly according to the voltage. Pieces of irregular dimensions can not easily be plated otherwise because, although by carefully computing the area an estimate of the current necessary to produce a certain average current density can be obtained, yet high points may be burned due to locally higher current densities. Some shapes are best plated by surrounding them by a loop of copper wire which acting as a "robber" takes the highest current densities and leaves the piece in an area of relatively constant current density.

Great ingenuity is displayed in designing the details of a plating installation such as the exhausting system, the connections between bus bars and anode or cathode rods, and in the racks for the work. Good electrical contacts are necessary everywhere. Some tanks are lined with reinforced, wired glass to prevent stray currents. Many such devices are making the control of a chrome-plating plant simpler and more satisfactory.

The greatest obstacle to the industry in the way of control has been the rather difficult methods of analysis. Methods have been proposed by Kruppa[o] and by Haring and Barrows.[99] Fortunately the composition of a bath does not fluctuate greatly nor change as rapidly as, for example, a nickel plating solution. The concentration of chromic acid can be determined by a rather simple titration and the proper additions can be made to the bath. On the other hand the analyses for trivalent chromium and iron are not quite so easy. Some of the work presented earlier in this bulletin has shown the concentration of trivalent chromium which can be expected under certain working conditions so that analysis for this element need be made but infrequently. If lead anodes are used, naturally no iron will enter the bath.

In the experiments described in this bulletin the hexavalent chromium was determined by an iodide titration with sodium thiosulphate. Trivalent chromium and iron were precipitated from a fresh sample with ammonia, dissolved and reprecipitated, separated with sodium hydroxide and hydrogen peroxide, dissolved and reseparated. The trivalent chromium now oxidized to the hexavalent state was titrated as above and the iron was redissolved, reprecipitated and ignited.

It was found expedient to make up the baths carefully to contain a certain concentration of sulphate rather than to analyze them later. The writers were unable to obtain results of even fair accuracy by a barium sulphate precipitation, either in the presence of chromates, or after the chromates had been reduced with alcohol, or with hydrogen peroxide in the presence of hydrochloric acid.

Sulphate analyses are both very necessary and rather difficult. If sulphate is precipitated with barium chloride, in the presence of hydrochloric acid, without first reducing the chromic acid, one or more of various possible results may take place:

1. Precipitation of some barium chromate if the solution is not sufficiently acid.
2. Solution of some barium sulphate if the solution is too acid.
3. Occlusion of chromates in the barium sulphate.

If, on the other hand, the chromates are first reduced, the problem resolves itself into a sulphate determination of a solution containing salts of

[o] Metallwaren-Industrie u. Galvanotechnik. January 15, 1926.
[99] Loc. cit.

trivalent chromium. This is not quite so simple as it seems. If the reduction is not complete, complex ions may affect the completeness of the precipitation of barium sulphate. If the reduction is complete there still remains the question of the modification of trivalent chromium so produced.

Chromic (trivalent) chromium exists in two modifications,[m] that is, it forms green salts and violet salts. When violet salts of chromium are dissolved in water, dissociation takes place in the normal manner giving Cr^{+++} and for example $SO_4^=$ or Cl^-. Precipitation of the anions will proceed normally with proper reagents.

If on the other hand the green chromium sulphate or chloride has been formed, it has been found that upon solution these salts ionize in a complex manner. Ions are produced containing chromium, hydroxyl, and chloride or sulphate. At 0°C. it has been found that barium chloride will not precipitate any sulphate and silver nitrate any chloride. Under most favorable conditions only two-thirds of the total sulphate or chloride can be precipitated.

It is most usual that salts of chromium will contain mixtures of the two modifications. In the present investigation a chemically pure chromium sulphate was analyzed for sulphate. Only 68.1 per cent of the theoretical sulphate could be precipitated with the usual procedure.

Weinland[n] found that the acetate ion is the most favorable anion toward the formation of violet chromium. Therefore, he carefully excludes as far as possible all other fixed anions when reducing chromates. In the present investigation chromic acid was reduced with tartaric acid in the presence of acetic acid. In this manner satisfactory sulphate analyses could be made. Work is still in progress on methods of analysis for chromic-acid baths.

A little work was done with an idea of removing trivalent chromium and iron, both detrimental to a plating bath.

It was found that the best way to reduce the trivalent chromium concentration when it has risen to too high a figure under the influence of iron anodes is to make a continuous electrolysis overnight, if convenient, with lead anodes. Such treatment will bring the trivalent chromium to a much lower figure.

Various attempts were made to remove iron. Iron is present as a colloidal iron hydroxide or chromate. Centrifuging with a force equal to 1,000

[m] Abegg. Handbuch der Anorganischen Chemie. Vol. 4, Part IV. 1, 2 page 146 ff. (1921). Also Savre and Valson, Comptes Rendus. 74: 1016, 1165 and 75: 798, 925, 1000 (1872).

[n] Komplexverbindungen. Second Edition, p. 391.

times that of gravity did not throw it down. Boiling a bath with powdered pumice did not remove iron. Boiling with chromic oxide, Cr_2O_3, which is insoluble in the bath, was found to remove 20 to 25 per cent of the dissolved iron.

A rapid method for removing lead chromate from lead anodes was developed. A saturated solution of sodium chloride, slightly acidulated with hydrochloric acid, readily dissolves lead chromate. If a treatment such as this could be given a lead anode periodically, the greatest drawback to the use of lead anodes would be overcome

Lukens[110] reports that excessive amounts of sulphate may be diminished by adding freshly prepared barium chromate. It is possible that barium hydroxide may be simpler to use and would prove as satisfactory. In the early parts of this investigation ordinary barium chromate was used, ineffectually as was later proven, as a buffer. However, this material did not precipitate any measurable amounts of sulphate.

Hardness of Chromium.

The great hardness of electrodeposited chromium noted by all investigators can be due to any one, or to a combination of the following factors:

1. The inherent character of the metal in a normal, annealed state.
2. Exceedingly small grain size.
3. The formation of alloys which are harder than the pure metal.
4. A condition of strain existing in the crystals.

In a brief study of the problem of hardness a number of specimens of plate were made in the following manner:

Brass tubes 1.5 centimeters in diameter were plated with chromium in a chromic-acid bath for 36 hours at 45°C. and a current density of 10 amperes per square decimeter. In this manner deposits of about a millimeter in thickness were obtained. The tubes were cut up into sections about 2 centimeters in length by means of a carborundum-rubber wheel. The base metal was dissolved away in nitric acid leaving small tubes of pure chromium metal.

A specimen was heated in boiling water for thirty hours; another at 200°C. for twenty-four hours; and other specimens were heated for twelve hours each at temperatures of 500, 700, 850, and 950°C., respectively, and were then tested with a file. The first two specimens, heated to 100°C. and 200°C. respectively were apparently just as hard as untreated specimens. The piece heated to 500°C. was colored purple and straw. It could be filed

[110] Trans. Am. Electrochem. Soc. 53: Preprint (1928).

but was still very hard. The other three specimens were oxidized and could be filed with comparative ease.

A specimen of unheated material was polished and etched. The structure is shown in Fig. 30. It is to be noted that the grain size is very small.

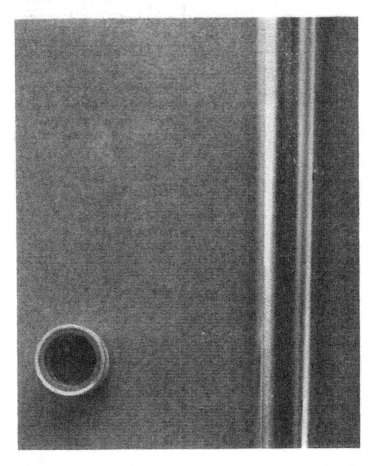

FIG. 30. This photograph shows the thickness and smoothness of the chromium deposit. In the cross section at the left the inner metal is brass and the outer, light colored metal is chromium. Actual size.

The presence of a strained condition in electrodeposited chromium has been demonstrated in several ways. Grant and Grant showed a system of cracks in plates of moderate commercial thickness and Baker and Pinner

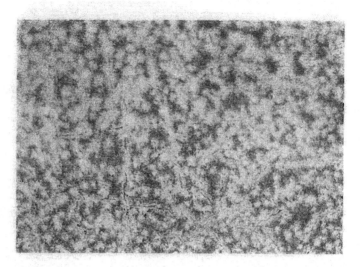

Fig. 31. Magnification 100. Etched with HCl. Typical structure of electrodeposited chromium. Most of the cracks were not visible in the specimen before etching. This metal was deposited at 10 amperes per square decimeter at 45°C.

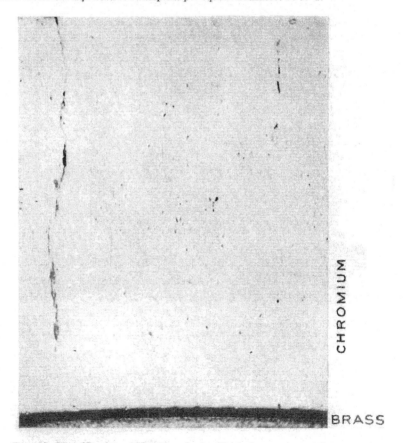

Fig. 32. Magnification 100. Unetched. Typical structure of electrodeposited chromium. Note the presence of a large number of voids. It seems that the frequency of voids is dependent upon plating conditions. Cracks can be seen in this specimen. The metal was deposited at 10 amperes per square decimeter at 45°C.

Fig. 33. Section at Right Angles to That in Figure 32. Magnification 100. Unetched. The voids in the deposit form patterns which are lines of weakness. Shock or mechanical stress will cause cracking along these lines.

Fig. 34. Magnification 100. Unetched. Cross section of heavy deposit of chromium deposited at 95 amperes per square decimeter at 85°C.

showed a system of very numerous fine cracks in thin deposits. Fig. 31 shows a portion of an unetched cross section of a deposit 1 millimeter thick formed at 45°C. at 10 amperes per square decimeter. This section was selected because it shows a number of voids characteristic of heavy deposits as can be seen in Fig. 32 which is at 100 diameters. In addition it shows the formation of a crack following along a group of voids. Although cracks

FIG. 35. Section at Right Angles to That in Figure 34. Magnification 100. Unetched. Note the exaggerated patterns in the chromium. This specimen to the naked eye presented a perfect appearance.

like this are rather infrequent, yet this would indicate the presence of great strains in the metal.

Figure 33 shows a section taken at right angles to the surface shown in Figure 31 and Figure 32. It can be seen that the voids form patterns along which cracking will occur if the metal is subjected to shock or stress.

Figures 34 and 35 show the structure of a cross-section and of a section parallel to the axis of the specimen respectively. This deposit differs from the previous one in that it was formed at 85°C. and 95 amperes per square decimeter. Conditions of plating of the two specimens were comparable in that the cathode current efficiencies were 13 per cent in each case. It can be seen that the structure has somewhat different characteristics from that in the plate deposited at 45°C. Voids seem to be less numerous but are larger in size.

These rather fragmentary observations would point out that the problem of hardness in chromium plate is a large subject upon which much work must be done before a tenable theory of the cause of hardness can be arrived at. A study of the voids and cracks in chromium plate also points out that judgment must be used in applying chromium for rust protective purposes.

CONCLUSIONS DRAWN FROM THE RESULTS OF RESEARCH

The problems in the electrodeposition of chromium from chromic-acid baths were studied by means of investigations along the following three general lines:

I. The effect of bath composition, nature of anodes, and plating conditions on the cathode deposit.

II. The effects of bath composition, nature of anodes, and plating conditions on anode behavior.

III. The effects of bath composition, nature of anodes, and plating conditions on the ultimate, "equilibrium," bath composition.

In addition some miscellaneous studies dealing with control methods and with some properties of electrodeposited chromium were made in a fourth section of the research.

The work presented in the foregoing portions of this bulletin has led to the following general conclusions:

Factors Affecting the Nature of the Deposit.

1. Of the two essential components of a chromic-acid plating bath, namely, chromic acid and sulphate ion, the concentration of the former may be varied over a wide range, but the concentration of the latter must be kept within very narrow limits.

2. The relative sulphate concentration expressed as the ratio by weight of hexavalent chromium to sulphate ion, $\frac{Cr^{VI}}{SO_4}$, must be maintained between 40 and 60.

3. For most favorable results, even with the above specified $\frac{Cr^{VI}}{SO_4}$ ratio,

the chromic-acid concentration should not be allowed to drop below 150 grams per liter. From the standpoint of throwing power and the extent of the bright-plating range, a concentration of about 350 grams per liter of chromic acid is somewhat advantageous. When other factors are considered, 250 grams per liter has been found commercially practicable. At 600 grams per liter a very narrow plating range results.

4. Trivalent chromium and iron in the amounts studied in the investigation, do not markedly affect the yield of chromium obtained at a given current density. Their presence does, however, greatly contract the range of current densities at which bright deposits can be obtained. It is believed that trivalent chromium has a much greater effect in this direction than has iron.

5. A low plating temperature, 15°C. or less, has a tendency, especially in the case of thin plates, to favor the deposition of a brown slime together with the metal. It is very difficult to obtain bright, shiny deposits at 15°C. from a solution which functions normally at temperatures above 25°C.

6. Too low or too high a cathode current density at a given temperature will result in milky or gray matte deposits respectively. For a given bath such a combination of cathode current density and temperature which results in a cathode current efficiency of 13 per cent gives the best deposits. For example, in a solution containing 250 grams per liter of chromic acid and 2.6 grams per liter of sulphate, at 45°C. (113°F.) a current density of 10 amperes per square decimeter (93 amperes per square foot) will produce good deposits. At any temperature, the current efficiency is a function of the logarithm of the current density.

7. The nature of the anode has no direct effect upon the cathode deposit. It may affect the composition of the bath which in turn can alter the characteristics of the deposit.

Factors Affecting the Anode Behavior.

1. A high sulphate concentration in the bath is conducive to a high rate of anode corrosion.

2. The most important determining factor in anode corrosion is the inherent chemical character of the anode material. It has been found by other investigators that iron or steel must be free from alloys such as nickel or chromium in order to be most resistant to corrosion as anodes.

3. Anodes tend to dissolve or corrode more rapidly at high temperatures than at low.

4. In the case of iron and steel anodes, very low anode current densities,

below 2.0 amperes per square decimeter (18 amperes per square foot) tend to increase the rate of corrosion markedly.

Factors Affecting the Equilibrium Bath Composition.

1. With fixed solution composition, anodes, and plating conditions such as current density and temperature, the trivalent chromium concentration of a chromic-acid plating bath will reach equilibrium. Naturally, in order to maintain every other factor constant, chromic acid and water must be added to the bath from time to time in order to replace the metal deposited out and the portion of the bath lost as spray or gas.

2. A high sulphate concentration of the bath favors a high equilibrium concentration of trivalent chromium.

3. The inherent nature of the anode material has probably a greater effect than has any other factor upon the magnitude of the equilibrium trivalent chromium concentration. This magnitude in turn is dependent upon the magnitude of the oxygen overvoltage of that metal or of its oxide. For example, anodes of lead, platinum, and iron are efficient in that order in keeping down the trivalent chromium concentration.

4. A high temperature favors a higher equilibrium trivalent chromium concentration, other things being equal.

5. A low anode current density, especially in the case of iron or steel anodes, causes a low equilibrium trivalent chromium concentration.

6. The equilibrium concentration of trivalent chromium is markedly higher in a bath in which electrolysis is very frequently interrupted than in one electrolyzed continuously.

Miscellaneous Conclusions.

1. Sulphate analyses are best carried out in acetate solutions rather than in chloride solutions.

2. Iron can not be satisfactorily removed from chromic-acid baths by any method known at the present time.

3. Lead chromate can readily be removed from lead anodes by means of a saturated solution of sodium chloride acidulated with hydrochloric acid.

4. Heavy chromium deposits show the presence of voids and cracks.

PART III

REVIEW OF THE LITERATURE
ON THE
ELECTRODEPOSITION OF METALLIC CHROMIUM

PART III

REVIEW OF THE LITERATURE ON THE ELECTRODEPOSITION OF METALLIC CHROMIUM

In presenting this review of the literature dealing with the electrodeposition of metallic chromium, but two phases will be taken up in detail; namely, the development of the processes of electrodeposition, and the theories underlying them. References have been obtained not only from the published scientific literature but also from the patent literature.

In the bibliography following this digest, completeness has been attempted for the period up to the year 1922 when the topic of chromium plating became very popular. Only the more important articles as contributing toward a knowledge of the processes of deposition, theory, or properties of the plate are considered. Detailed information on patent references has been published in a previous Engineering Research bulletin entitled, "A Study of Patents Dealing with the Electrodeposition of Chromium."

Processes for Electrodepositing Metallic Chromium.

The history of the processes for electrodeposition of metallic chromium necessarily can not extend very far back in the history of chemistry because the Voltaic pile was not evolved until 1792, and chromium was not discovered by Vauquelin until 1797. The earliest electrolysis of water was not performed until 1800, when Nicholson and Carlisle successfully separated water into its constituents. By 1834, however, there was sufficient data on the electrolytic deposition of metals and non-metals that Faraday was able to formulate the fundamental laws of electrolysis.

The earliest record of the electrolytic deposition of metallic chromium comes to light in a British patent granted to Junot in 1852. A French patent had been applied for in 1847 by the same investigator. However, the present writer has not seen the application and therefore can not state whether or not the patent was granted. In the specifications of the British patent Junot describes the deposition of metallic chromium from a bath consisting of "Chromium dissolved in a double chloride of soda and ammonia in the proportion of about one hundred grams of metal to one Kilogram of the salt dissolved in ten liters of water." Electrolysis was carried on at 30 to 40°C. between platinum anodes. Details of the process are so vague that it is doubtful whether his results can readily be duplicated.

Bunsen successfully deposited chromium in a two-compartment electrolyzing cell. For the anode he used a hollow carbon vessel containing acid. A platinum cathode was immersed in the electrolyte in the cathode chamber. The plating bath consisted of a concentrated solution of a chromous chloride which contained a little chromic salt. Electrolysis was carried out at boiling temperature with a cathode current density of about 65 amperes per square decimeter (approximately 610 amperes per square foot).

It may be interesting to quote directly from the English translation of the article which appeared in 1854:

> "Chromium and manganium (manganese) are thus separated with the greatest facility from their chloruretted solutions, provided that the negative pole is small and the saline solution very concentrated; if not, we may, at will, obtain hydrogen, peroxide or protoxide of chromium, or chromoso-chromic oxide. When the galvanic deposit is formed only of these oxides, it is sufficient to add solid protochloride of chromium to obtain metallic chromium.
>
> "In this state the chrome is chemically pure; it presents the appearance of iron, but it is less alterable by humid air. Heated in the air, it is converted into sesquioxide. It resists nitric acid even when boiling, hydrochloric and aqueous sulphuric acids act on it forming a proto-salt. The density of galvanic chromium coincides with the density deduced from the atomic volumes, and does not differ much from the known density. . . . .
>
> "On diminishing the current, the metal ceases to be deposited, and in its place appears a black powder, not crystalline, anhydrous, formed of protoxide and sesquioxide of chromium; the composition of this powder varies between the formula $2CrO + Cr_2O_3$ and $3CrO + Cr_2O_3$; it is insoluble in the acids, it is purified by boiling it in aqua regia, it burns vividly in the air.
>
> "Prof. Bunsen obtained sheets of chromium of more than fifty square millimeters surface; these sheets were friable, and presented a perfect polish on the side which had been in contact with the platinum."

A few years later Geuther, by electrolyzing solutions of chromic acid between platinum electrodes, obtained deposits of metallic chromium. At the same time he noted evolution of hydrogen at the cathode and of oxygen at the anode. The volume of oxygen liberated proved to be greater than would be predicted by Faraday's law.

Attempts to repeat Geuther's work resulted in different conclusions. Buff, while proving the evolution of oxygen at the anode perfectly normal, was unable to obtain any metal. On the other hand Bartoli and Papasogli obtained metallic chromium in confirmation of Geuther. They described their plate as being very tenacious and of great brilliancy (tenacissimo, splendidissimo) and as having been deposited from chromium chromate. This chromium chromate was a by-product in the electrolysis.

Slater showed that alloys of chromium with platinum, gold, nickel, copper, and other metals were capable of being electrodeposited.

In 1890, and continuing for several years, Placet and Bonnet obtained patents for chromium-plating baths containing chromic salts, mixtures of chromic salts with various other salts and acids, or chromic acid or alkali chromates.

The American patent granted in 1894 contains probably a summation of their various European claims. The electrolyte described in their first descriptive paragraph is as follows:

"A solution of chromic acid in water. This solution may be very little concentrated. One to two grams of chromic acid in one hundred grams of water are sufficient. However, the more the solution is concentrated, the more abundant is the deposition. We vary the shade of the metal deposited by adding to the solution a small quantity (for example—five to ten grams per liter) of one of the following acids: phosphoric, sulphurous, oxalic, benzoic, formic, gallic, pyrogallic, picric, phenic, salicylic, and other analogous acids.

"Similarly the solution may be made up in the following manner:

"To a solution of chromic acid, of chromate or bichromate of an alkali metal, we add a small quantity of any acid (sulphuric acid, chlorhydric, phosphoric, or other). We add, further, a sulphate, a chloride, or other alkaline salt; and we obtain a bath which is very easily reducible by electricity. We take for example—ten to fifteen grams of an alkaline bi-chromate, five to ten grams of any suitable acid, fifteen to twenty grams of chrome-alum, and one hundred grams of water. We add sometimes a little alcohol or any other reducing body, to render the reaction more rapid."

The chromic acid used was either ordinary chromic acid of commerce or some that was formed by adding a suitable acid to an alkali chromate or dichromate and electrolyzing with the use of a diaphragm.

Placet and Bonnet in the same patent described the use of electrolytes containing chromic salts and alums which were acidulated by various optional means. Salts of alkali or alkali-earth metals were added to assist deposition. Bath potentials of 30 to 40 volts were described.

Alloys of chromium were obtainable, they said, by adding oxides or carbonates of other metals such as tungsten, molybdenum, copper, nickel, or iron to a bath of either of the above types.

The use of fuzed electrolytes was also described in detail.

Unfortunately, this work was not readily capable of duplication probably because the specifications were not sufficiently detailed. Le Blanc was unable to obtain more than faintest traces of metal by following the directions in the Placet and Bonnet patents.

For various reasons, investigators seemed to find it even more difficult to deposit chromium from chromic acid than from chromic salts. At any rate although little work was done with chromic-acid baths, the literature of the period up to about 1905 is rich in descriptions of the use of chromic salt baths.

Marino obtained a patent covering a solution similar to those of Placet and Bonnet. It was prepared as follows:

"A solution containing one equivalent of sulphate of chromium is mixed with a solution containing less than one equivalent of chloride of calcium. An insoluble precipitate of sulphate of calcium is obtained, and a solution of chloride of chrome with chromsulphate in it, which will deposit chrome when set to action."

Later he changed the composition of the bath.

In a British patent a method is given for the electrolytic deposition of aluminum, glucinum, antimony, chromium, palladium, lead, vanadium, zinc, gold, tin, copper, nickel, cobalt, manganese, and iron. For the deposition of aluminum or chromium, an excess of caustic potash is added to a solution of salt of the metal. To a solution of an alkaline phosphate or pyrophosphate, barium chloride or nitrate is added. The resulting precipitate is dissolved in hydrochloric acid. The two solutions are mixed, the resulting precipitate of barium hydroxide is removed, and the filtrate is ready for electrolysis.

Moeller and Street described a two-cell apparatus in the cathode chamber of which an electrolyte was used containing equal parts by weight of chrome alum, sodium sulphate, and water. Electrolysis was carried on with lead anodes at 70°C. at a cathode current density of 40 amperes per square decimeter. The yield proved to be 30 per cent of the theoretical. Using a very similar apparatus Boehringer and Sons obtained only chromous salts, but Goldschmidt, on the other hand, obtained metal.

Cowper-Coles was able to obtain very good yields of metal by electrolyzing a 25-per-cent solution of chromic chloride acidulated with hydrochloric acid. He operated at 75 to 85°C., at 4.3–5.3 amperes per square decimeter (40 to 50 amperes per square foot) with a potential of 4 volts. The deposit was found to possess a high reflecting power and a good resistance to tarnish. On an arbitrary scale in which the hardness of electrodeposited nickel was 10 and cadmium 4.5, this chromium possessed a hardness of 7.

By proper additions of hydrochloric acid or potassium chloride to strong solutions of chromic chloride, Férée was also able to obtain metal in yields of about 45 per cent of the theoretical. Cathode current density was given as 15 amperes per square decimeter. At low current densities nothing but hydrogen was produced. Upon electrolyzing a 16-per-cent solution of chromium chloride alone, he was able to obtain only deposits of chromic oxide.

Glaser, working under the direction of Neumann, electrolyzed many solutions of chromic sulphate, chloride, and acetate. Solutions of these salts were placed in the cathode chamber and mineral acids were used in the anode compartment. Under some conditions they readily obtained deposits of metallic chromium while at others at the cathode various oxides of chromium, hydrogen, or mixtures of these were produced.

Carveth and Mott becoming attracted by the industrial possibilities of pure chromium studied exhaustively the deposition of chromium metal from solutions of its trivalent salts. It was found necessary to duplicate much of the older work because, with the exception of Glaser's research, most of the information published had been more or less fragmentary or presented very elementary, pioneer work.

A systematic study was made in which the catholyte consisted of chromic chloride, sulphate, and oxalate respectively. The effects of varying the catholyte concentration and temperature were noted. It was found that by rotating the cathode higher current densities could be used. Agitating the bath with air, however, tended to lower the current efficiency. The composition and concentration of the anolyte was varied and the effects noted.

Following is their summary of conclusions:

"(1) The presence of chromous salt appears to be essential to the successful deposition of the metal from its chloride or sulphate solutions. This has been proved by showing, (a) that the current does work in reducing the chromic to the chromous salts; (b) that it is necessary to electrolyze the chromic salts for some time before the metal can be deposited with any considerable efficiency; and (c) that the efficiency is destroyed by oxidation of the chromous salt.

"(2) Temperature has a very decided influence upon the efficiency of deposition; this result is in direct opposition to those recorded by Neumann. For each especial set of conditions there seems to be a temperature at which the loss in efficiency caused by the decomposition of the chromous salt is balanced by increased efficiency caused by other factors. As might be predicted, the more concentrated the solution, the higher the temperature which may be advantageously employed.

"(3) The nature of the anode solution affects the yield very considerably;

that this is probably due to the diffusion of the anolyte into the cathode chamber is indicated by the peculiar results obtained in the continued efficiency runs.

"(4) On continued electrolysis of the solutions of chromic salts, the efficiency rises from zero to a value which is practically constant. This may be accounted for by assuming that the absolute and relative masses of the chromous and chromic salts have, under the conditions employed, become practically constant in the solution. Any factor tending to change these relations will affect the current efficiency—for example, change of temperature, increase of acidity, change of concentration and the presence of catalytic agents such as toluene or petroleum ether.

"(5) In the ordinary problems of electrochemistry, it is conceivable that in reducing from the higher stages of oxidation, that solution from which metal can be deposited may not be obtained. For this reason solutions in which the metal shows its lowest valency should in this and in all analogous cases be used when it is desired to obtain good current efficiencies in the deposition of metal.

"We have also noted that the quality of the deposit is always bad when the current efficiency is less than five per cent; an acid bath favors hard and strong deposits but causes lower efficiencies."

Subsequent to this paper very little can be found in the literature dealing with the deposition of chromium from chromic-salt baths. Due to the higher current yields obtainable and the lower current densities required than is the case in chromic-acid baths, this process will always have an interest for the commercial plater. With few exceptions, however, attempts to plate chromium by this method on a large scale have not been successful. One of the greatest drawbacks in the development of this process has been the difficulty of obtaining chromium anodes and chromium salts at a price sufficiently low to make it attractive. In addition, the plating industry is rather prejudiced against the use of diaphragms. Processes in which the diaphragm is omitted have not been uniformly successful.

Among discussions on the properties of chromic salts Abegg states that these salts occur in two modifications: violet and green. The violet modification in solution ionizes normally and electrodeposition can readily be made to take place. The green modification of the sulphate, on the other hand, ionizes to form a complex cation containing chromium, hydroxyl and a part of the sulphate. In this case only hydrogen will be deposited upon electrolysis. The stability of the two modifications is influenced by temperature, acidity, and other factors. Most salts will be found to exist as a combination of these two forms.

Askenasy and Revai, however, were unable to find any difference in the reducibility of the green and violet chrome alums.

It must be recalled in taking up the subject of chromic-acid baths that

Geuther's deposition of metal from a chromic-acid solution was confirmed by Bartoli and Papasogli, and Placet and Bonnet although Buff was unable to obtain any metal whatsoever. Reese was unable even to reduce chromic acid to a form of lower valence by electrolysis in the absence of sulphates.

Carveth and Curry systematically and thoroughly investigated the results of previous workers. They started with pure chromic acid and found that by using a higher voltage than Reese they were able to reduce chromic acid.

With a 14.28-per-cent solution of chromic acid containing 0.01 per cent of sulphate impurity at 20°C. and at an anode and cathode current density of 125 amperes per square decimeter, they obtained a 90.2-per-cent yield of hydrogen and an 8.37-per-cent yield of chromium. At 90°C. under otherwise identical conditions the hydrogen efficiency was 99.8 per cent and that of chromium 0.5 per cent. The last figure is probably in error due to difficulty in determining the deposit which was reported as 0.0002 gram.

Using at 20°C. 50 cubic centimeters of a 14.28-per-cent solution of chromic acid plus 1 per cent of sulphuric acid with the same current densities as before they obtained the following yields in successive electrolyses:

	TIME	PER CENT HYDROGEN DEFICIENCY	Mg. Cr.	PER CENT HYDROGEN EFFICIENCY	PER CENT CHROMIUM EFFICIENCY	PER CENT EFFICIENCY OF OXYGEN DEPOSITION
	seconds					
1	930	66.2	15.2	33.8	36.1	82.3
2	935	62.7	19.8	37.3	47.1	81.8
3	510	55.5	11.4	44.5	50.2	84.3
4	3,600 570	52.8	6.4	47.2	25.0	89.5
5	7,200 535	1.2	3.0	98.8	12.5	94.4

The actual current was 0.5 ampere; platinum electrodes were used. The variations in yields in successive runs were due to the rapid impoverishment of the bath which in turn was due to the small volume, 50 cubic centimeters.

In the above table the present writer has calculated the last three columns from the data. The per cent hydrogen efficiency has been assumed as 100 per cent minus the per cent reduction or hydrogen deficiency given by Carveth and Curry. The per cent chromium efficiency has been calculated on the basis of a hexavalent ion.

It is to be noted that, by adding the two cathode efficiencies, 100 per cent is not obtained. This discrepancy is probably accounted for by the fact that part of the hydrogen while in its nascent state reacts with chromic acid to form trivalent chromium.

Electrolysis Number 5 was conducted when the metal content of the bath had been reduced to one half of its original value. The sum of the cathode efficiencies of hydrogen and chromium equals 111.3 per cent. It is probable that most of the metal was deposited from the trivalent ion instead of the hexavalent ion due to the great change in solution composition. This would account for the apparent abnormal figure.

The oxygen efficiency is less than 100 per cent in all cases. Trivalent chromium being oxidized at the anode is the probable explanation for this.

With a lead anode of the same area the oxygen efficiency was lowered while the hydrogen efficiency increased.

Electrolyses were made of chromic-acid baths containing other sulphates, chlorides, nitrates, and chromates. Fixed anions proved more satisfactory than those which were decomposed or deposited by the current.

In regard to the function of these additions of "impurities" they write:

"Why does the sulphuric acid increase the efficiency? It is well recognized by electrochemists that the efficiency of a metal deposition varies very considerably with the number of ions of the metal present in the solution. With a small number, low efficiencies are expected; as this number increases, the efficiency will increase. We suggest, therefore, that the sulphuric acid has increased the number of chromium cations in the solution. It is probable that in its presence, the dissociation of the chromic acid is forced back to the CrO_3 stage and that the secondary dissociation of this into hexavalent chromium cations is thereby increased.

"Another method of expressing the same result is this—when sulphuric acid reacts with CrO_3, the latter behaves as a base, and hexavalent chromium tends to be formed, although normally the trivalent salt is the more stable form. It does not seem at all improbable therefore that the various acids and also various salts tend to increase the ionization of chromic acid to hexavalent ions, and that this effect is shown in the increase of efficiency of deposition of the metal."

The presence of chromium chromate was found to cause a very decided decrease in the yield of metal.

They summed up their conclusions as follows:

"This evidence therefore makes it seem very probable that in chromic acid there exists a number of hexavalent chromium cations in equilibrium with many other ions, and that chromium in chromic acid may be considered a reversible electrode.

"The main part of the work of Geuther is correct. Metallic chromium is deposited in the electrolysis of solutions of chromic acid, but this requires a high current density, which in this case is synonymous with a high decomposition voltage.

"The results of Buff are readily understood when the current density he employed is calculated. Under no conditions have we been able to get deposition of the metal at a current density as low as he used; nor have we with any but very impure acids been able to duplicate his results.

"Like Buff, the other workers, Schick, Cowper-Coles and Féreé have probably used too low current densities; it seems very improbable that their materials were purer than those used in the investigation.

"Some of the claims of Placet and Bonnet are sound. It is very probable that solutions of commercial chromic acid and of chromates to which have been added various substances which aid in the reduction may not be used in a continuous and economical process for the extraction of chromium, since the efficiency is so rapidly decreased by the formation of the reduction products. By oxidizing these, however, it would be possible to continue the extraction of metal, making the process continuous. There is nothing to prevent the use of this method in the laboratory for the purpose of making pure chromium.

"By selection of the proper impurity (e.g., sulphuric acid) we have been able in a continued electrolysis to recover in the metallic form more than half the total chromium present in the solution. Had the reduced products been oxidized, this yield could have been carried to any limits desired.

"Electrolytic chromium may occlude as much as two hundred and fifty times its volume of hydrogen.

"It is possible to reduce chromic acid to the trivalent chromic salts in the presence of an excess of a mineral acid."

In another printing of this paper they describe the deposit as follows:

"Platings made without stirring the solution and without finishing by buffing, etc., resemble the very finest work done with silver. In fact, for plating purposes the metal should have a great future before it."

In the discussion after the paper had been read they exhibited a piece of chromium plated metal which had been severely twisted. The plate had neither cracked nor flaked off. In a discussion of Le Blanc's paper in 1906, Curry reported a good chromium deposit of over a millimeter in thickness.

Carveth and Curry's conclusions as to the essential constituents in the bath were further confirmed by Askenasy and Revai and by Baum's success in obtaining chromium through selection of the proper current density from chromic-acid baths containing either chromic sulphate or boric acid.

Sargent working at the same institution as had Carveth and Curry extended their research in a manner such that their results became more directly usable to the plating industry. He determined the effect of varying bath temperature, cathode current density, chromic acid concentration, and sulphate concentration upon the nature and amount of the cathode deposit. He favored a higher concentration of chromic acid than had Carveth and Curry and adjusted his chromic sulphate concentration so that deposition of metal at a given temperature was affected at the lowest possible current densities.

A deposit 1.15 centimeters thick was deposited from a solution containing 25 per cent of chromic acid and 0.3 per cent chromic sulphate. The current density was 10 amperes per square decimeter and the temperature 20°C. If the solutions were made up by weight the chromic acid concentration proves to be 300 grams per liter if specific gravity is considered.

Sargent differs from Carveth and Curry in his theoretical conclusions. He noticed the formation of trivalent chromium in the bath and this fact led him to use chromic sulphate as the addition agent rather than sulphuric acid. The trivalent chromium forms a cathode film of chromium chromate, he says, behind which chromium is deposited from a di- or trivalent ion. This conception is in accord with the views of Bartoli and Papasogli.

Regarding this view he says:

"The theory of the deposition of chromium from chromic acid-chromic sulphate solutions seems to be first the formation of a film of basic chromic chromate on the cathode with a very weak acid solution in contact with the cathode. Then there is a partial reduction of chromic ions to chromous ions and the deposition of chromium from both chromous and chromic ions together with an abundant evolution of hydrogen. The chromous ions also react with the film or with the chromic acid outside the film, causing the reduction of a considerable amount of chromic acid.

"The formation of a film on the cathode is almost always accompanied with a sudden increase in the voltage between the electrodes and by the sudden evolution of hydrogen at the cathode. The film can be obtained in almost any chromic acid solution. It is a brown substance, which has been obtained by Geuther, Buff, Morges, and Carveth and Curry.

"Strong C. P. chromic acid solutions are reduced practically quantitatively with low current densities in the absence of a cathode film. At higher current densities a cathode film forms and then hydrogen is evolved quantitatively. At very high current densities chromium may be deposited and chromic acid reduced.

"Strong chromic acid solutions containing small amounts of chromic sulphate are reduced quantitatively with low current densities in the absence of a cathode film. At higher current densities a cathode film forms and then chromium may be deposited, chromic acid reduced, and hydrogen evolved. With very small amounts of chromic sulphate present hydrogen is evolved quantitatively at the current density at which the cathode film forms but at higher current density chromium begins to be deposited and chromic acid reduced."

He sums up his experience with anodes in the following statement:

"When lead anodes are used practically all the chromic acid reduced at the cathode is oxidized back to chromic acid at the anode.

"This makes it possible to maintain the composition of the plating solution desired for an indefinite length of time.

"The use of ferro-chromium anodes as a cheap source of chromium for plating or refining is impracticable owing to the lack of a process for removing the iron periodically from the plating solution without adding an equally objectionable substance."

In closing Sargent pointed out that chromium plating had commercial possibilities owing to its extreme resistance to corrosion by air, moisture, and many chemicals.

All this work was done in 1912 or 1913 under the direction of Prof. W. D. Bancroft although the paper was not presented until 1920. In 1920 about a month before the paper was presented Liebreich published a theoretical treatise in which he propounded a theory similar in many respects to that of Sargent. The greatest point of difference lay in their cathode current density—cathode potential curves.

Sargent found one break at which he reported that "hydrogen is evolved, chromium is deposited, and chromic acid is reduced." Liebreich, on the other hand, found three distinct breaks in his curve. Up to the first there was no hydrogen evolution and no metal deposition; chromic acid was reduced. After the break in the curve there was still no hydrogen; chromic chromate was formed. After the second break there was a feeble evolution of hydrogen and the formation of chromous chromite. After the last break, corresponding to the one Sargent found, there was a strong evolution of hydrogen accompanied by deposition of chromium metal. Müller in an article published in 1926 agreed with Sargent and Liebreich that the film at the cathode was composed of chromic oxide or chromate, but believed that metal deposition occurs from a hexavalent ion. According to his theory, the sulphate present in a bath tends to destroy the film and allow chromic acid to reach the cathode and be reduced there. Liebreich's commercial solutions consisted of chromic acid plus trivalent chromium; sulphate was not mentioned. This point will be discussed later.

Although Carveth and Curry had shown that chromium was readily electrodeposited from a solution containing chromic acid and an ion such as sulphate, Salzer in 1907 obtained a patent for a bath of the following nature:

The plating bath consists of a solution of chromic acid, CrO_3; and chromoxid, Cr_2O_3, in a ratio of 2:1. However, a ratio closer to 1:1 is advised. The solution may contain the equivalent of from 5 per cent to 25 per cent metallic chromium.

"The bath may be prepared:

"1. By the partial reduction of chromic acid by electrolysis or by chemical means.

"2. By a partial saturation of chromic acid, CrO_3, with chromium hydroxide, $Cr(OH)_3$.

"3. By the partial oxidation of (trivalent) chromium salts.

"To increase the conductivity the presence of a small amount of an electrolyte, sulphuric acid for example, will be advantageous. . . . .

"Cathodic current density will be from 2 to 5 amperes per square decimeter (about 18 to 45 amperes per square foot) at room temperature."

Variations are mentioned.

The anodes should be insoluble, such as fused iron oxide, lead, or platinum. A diaphragm might or might not be used.

Salzer pointed out the advisability of watching and controlling the concentration of dissolved electrolyte and of controlling the temperature. A few years later Salzer described more rapid deposition and more firm plate by adding chromic sulphate to his original bath.

In both cases, however, he stated that the chromium chromate formed was the active compound which promoted metal deposition. Liebreich's work was much along the same line. All of the baths he described or patented were characterized by the presence of trivalent chromium. Both Salzer and Liebreich differ from Sargent in that they consider sulphate merely an aid in promoting conductivity. In later work Liebreich showed that deposition was accomplished at lower current densities in the presence of sulphates but the wording of his various articles and patents would indicate that trivalent chromium is the essential addition to a chromic-acid bath.

Sargent's results, however, have since been amply confirmed both in laboratory experiments and in commercial work. Schwartz obtained bright deposits on steel at 10 amperes per square decimeter from the solution Sargent recommended. He used chromium anodes. Winkler, Sigrist, and Wantz carefully checked Sargent and reported the following results with the use of a concentrated bath:

1. Minimum voltage for deposition: 3.4 volts.

2. Yield at 160 amperes per square decimeter at room temperature: 0.16–0.17 g./amp. hour.

3. The best coherent deposit was obtained without heat by a low current density.

4. The state of the cathode surface such as polish is of great consequence.

5. The time duration of the electrolysis is unimportant to the quality of the deposit.

6. The presence of chromium sulphate is indispensable.

7. Ferric salts, calcium and sodium sulphates reduced the yield and deteriorated the quality of the plate.

Fink confirmed the statement that chromium sulphate is an indispensible addition to chromic acid. He went a step farther in showing, however, that the sulphate ion was the important factor and that any sulphate would be equally well. He pointed out that equivalent amounts of other acid radicals added either as acids or soluble salts functioned satisfactorily. This is quite in agreement with Carveth and Curry's conclusions and has been again confirmed by Müller and by Haring and Barrows.

In practice Sargent's solution has been mentioned as the means of obtaining electrodeposited chromium upon tools, wearing surfaces of machinery, inner surfaces of oil cracking equipment, golf clubs, and other articles which in the finished, plated condition are protected by patents. By Sargent's bath usually is meant the bath from which he deposited a plate 1.15 centimeters thick; this contained 25 per cent CrO_3 and 0.3 per cent $Cr_2(SO_4)_3$; similar baths naturally give similar results. It is clear, therefore, that the bath has been successful commercially when prepared and used properly.

The fact that Salzer and Liebreich both reported successful chromium deposition from a bath containing essentially chromic acid and trivalent chromium with sulphate as an optional addition and Sargent's statement that metal could not be deposited directly from a hexavalent ion aided in causing a turning away from Carveth and Curry's conclusions. Another disturbing factor lay in the difficulty of procuring pure chemicals. Although "C.P." chromic acid was procurable which would contain about 0.25 per cent sulphate impurity or less, technical grades varied almost unbelievably in composition. The present writer obtained a sample sold in 1920 as ordinary commercial chromic acid whose analysis showed 23.35 per cent of hexavalent chromium and 27.06 per cent sulphate. A sulphate content of 2 to 5 per cent was not unusual. This coupled with the difficulty in analyzing chromic acid solutions and with conflicting statements as to the essential components in a bath led to great confusion.

It was not unusual for a worker attempting to reproduce Sargent's results with commercial chemicals to meet with failure. Baths were proposed in which the amount of sulphate added was lower than Sargent found best and to which "buffers" such as chromium hydroxide, chromium carbonate, chromium oxide, copper carbonate, and other such materials were added. These solutions were clearly compromises in which both Carveth and Curry's and Liebreich's ideas were combined. The apparent low sulphate concentration was unwittingly increased by impurities in the other chemicals.

The subject of buffers attracted a great deal of attention until Haring and Barrows proved conclusively that the only effect these materials could exert upon a bath was to introduce more sulphate or similar ion as an impurity. The pH of a 2.5 molar bath is less than 1 and small amounts of chromium hydroxide, usually less than 50 per cent soluble, can not materially change the acidity.

Haring and Barrows also amplified the work of Carveth and Curry and of Sargent so that not only was the best solution composition determined but also optimum plating conditions were given for several metal cathode materials. They discussed methods of plant and chemical control.

Aside from their discussion of anodes and that of Watts mentioned on page 44 most of the later outstanding published articles deal with the properties and uses of chromium plate.

Adcock, Schischkin and Gernet, and Grant and Grant showed that electrodeposited chromium exhibits a marked tendency toward cracking. If corrosion takes place under the plate, it will tend to lift the deposit upward in flakes bounded by the cracks.

The cracks described by these investigators occurred in comparatively heavy plate and gave the appearance on superficial examination of being huge grain boundaries. Baker and Pinner found another system of fine cracks appearing on very thin layers of chromium plate. These cracks destroyed the value of the deposit as a corrosion-resisting material. They found that upon increasing the thickness of plate up to a certain point, the corrosion resistance increased. This was due to a gradual closing up of pores in the deposit. At about 500 ampere minutes per square foot a maximum corrosion resistance was observed. Heavier plate was less resistant due to the fact that fine parallel cracks were formed. These cracks were probably due to strains set up in the chromium during deposition. When the amount of plate is several times the thickness mentioned in the paper naturally these fine cracks tended to grow shut and the larger, less frequent cracks shown by Grant and Grant develop.

Baker and Pinner go on and say:

"Chromium has little protective value for outdoor exposure when applied directly to steel, within the range of thickness covered by these experiments, when compared with the protective value that might be obtained for the same cost if combination coatings were used.

"Copper under chromium is inferior to the same thickness of nickel under chromium, and, in fact, in thickness up to 0.0003 in. the combination has little to recommend it. A base coating consisting of 200 nickel and 300 "acid" copper likewise gives disappointingly low results.

"The combination of 100 nickel, 100 "acid" copper, and 300 nickel under chromium, strangely enough, is not superior to 300 nickel under chromium. This agrees, in general, with some results reported by Baker and by Blum and Thomas, which also indicate that very thin alternate deposits of nickel and copper have little protective value. Presumably, in such a case, no one layer is thick enough to be non-porous.

"The best results for any of the combinations tried were obtained with a base coating of 200 nickel, 300 copper, and 400 nickel, which gives the highest values when used alone and when covered with chromium."

The numbers 100, 200, and 300 are arbitrary measures for the thickness of copper and nickel deposits and are described in the paper as being the number of ampere-minutes per square foot of cathode.

Ollard had some years previously determined qualitatively the relative corrosion-resisting values of chromium plate, alone and in combination with other metals. His data is so valuable that it will be given in full.

The Effect of Underlying Metals.

"Combinations of nickel, copper, cadmium and chromium were used, the platings being done by a semi-skilled assistant in baths that were being used for various other plating operations, under the ordinary conditions. The various groups of test pieces were plated in the following manner:

"*Group 1.* One hour deposited in a cadmium cyanide bath.
"*Group 2.* Three hours deposited in a nickel sulphate bath.
"*Group 3.* Half-an-hour deposited in cadmium cyanide bath and one hour in nickel sulphate bath.
"*Group 5.* One hour in nickel sulphate bath and half-an-hour in cadmium cyanide bath.
"*Group 6.* One hour in nickel sulphate bath, one hour in copper sulphate bath, then buffed and plated half-an-hour in nickel sulphate bath.
"*Group 7.* Half-an-hour in chromium bath.
"*Group 8.* Half-an-hour in copper cyanide bath followed by half-an-hour in chromium bath.
"*Group 9.* One hour in cadmium cyanide bath followed by half-an-hour in chromium bath.
"*Group 10.* One hour in nickel bath followed by half-an-hour in chromium bath.

"*Group 11.* Half-an-hour in copper cyanide bath followed by one hour in copper sulphate bath.

"*Group 12.* Two hours in nickel bath followed by half-an-hour in chromium bath.

"The test pieces plated in this manner were then tested as described above. The difficulty in testing pieces of this nature lies in the fact that if the outer plating has been removed in any part, the rate of corrosion is materially changed and usually very much accelerated. Test pieces of this nature show three types of failure. In the first case the coatings are gradually and fairly evenly removed until finally the base metal is exposed, after which corrosion takes place very rapidly; in the second the plating is originally either pitted or somewhat porous and corrosion takes place at a few local spots, while in the third case the plating is thrown off from the metal underneath it, either because it does not adhere or because the underlying metal is corroded through the pores of the outer one.

"The test pieces were all measured and weighed before and after the tests and the loss of weight per unit area was calculated. Notes of the appearance of the test piece were also kept and specimens of one of each of the groups exposed on the roof."

Roof Test.

"The specimens were hung from a frame on the roof of the laboratory, suspended directly above a trough of water and exposed to the Trafford Park atmosphere. The time allowed for this test was 768 hours and examinations were made at intervals.

"Under these conditions the nickel plated specimens were readily attacked and showed a greenish deposit on the surface. The cadmium specimen stood fairly well but appeared to be evenly attacked. The copper specimen was very much tarnished and also lost a good deal of weight. In the case of the chromium deposited directly on to steel, chromium plating was almost entirely removed having apparently been thrown off by the corrosion of the steel underneath it. The chromium deposits, however, which have been made on copper and nickel stood quite satisfactorily with only slight traces of local rusting. In the case of chromium deposited on to cadmium, this specimen stood remarkably well but in some places the chromium flaked away from the cadmium coating. The chromium plating does not appear to adhere well to the cadmium, and, especially in the subsequent tests which involve temperature rise, the chromium plating was almost entirely removed from the cadmium. The most satisfactory specimen from the point of view of loss in weight was that in which the steel was first copper and then chromium plated (8) although those with nickel as an underlying metal (10 and 12) also stood very well.

Salt Spray Test.

"As chromium is attacked very violently by hydrochloric acid it was thought that the conditions prevailing in the salt spray would corrode it very rapidly. This point is rather an important one as claims have been made that chromium plated material will withstand the action of sea water and this is a big factor in its industrial application. It was found, however, that the salt spray had very much less action on the chromium plating than was anticipated, and it is thought that probably a definite pH value of the solution is required before the chromium is readily attacked. The pH value of the solution used in the salt spray was about 6.4 being slightly on the acid side; (sea-water about 6.6). It is thought probable that this is slightly more acid than the sea water and it is proposed to make tests with sea water and also by exposing the test piece to marine condition.

"The specimens were sprayed for 122 hours of actual spraying, being examined at intervals and allowed to remain in the chamber at night, while the spray was not working.

"In this test the most satisfactory platings were those consisting of both nickel and cadmium (3 and 5). The chromium plating with nickel and an underlying metal stood quite satisfactorily, losing about the same weight as the nickel plated specimens and less than the cadmium plated specimen. The copper plated specimen (11) was very badly corroded.

Heat Test.

"One specimen of each group was heated intermittently in an oven at about 400°C. to 420°C for 150 hours of actual heating. Weights in this case were rather difficult to interpret, as, in some cases, there was a definite gain in weight due to oxidisation. In this case, again the cadmium plated samples (1) were badly attacked and also the chromium plated on cadmium (9). In this latter case the chromium was almost entirely thrown off.

"The other chromium plated samples all seemed to stand well, the surface of the plating, however, oxidising slightly. The nickel plated specimen (2) also stood well.

"Another test piece of steel was made which was plated first with nickel for about an hour, then an hour in the copper sulphate bath, then replated with nickel for half-an-hour, polished, and finally chromium plated for half-an-hour. This specimen was exposed on the roof of the chemical laboratory for about three months and at the end of this time was still quite bright, showing no apparent sign of rusting. Weights in this case were not taken."

In taking a broad historical view of the whole development of the process for electrodeposition of metallic chromium from chromic-acid baths, three major accomplishments became apparent;

I. Geuther showed that chromium could be deposited from a bath whose principal constituent was chromic acid.

II. Carveth and Curry determined the essential components of the bath. Solutions of chemically pure chromic acid need the addition of small amounts of "impurity" such as sulphuric acid, sodium sulphate, nitric acid, hydrochloric acid, sodium chloride, sodium dichromate or some acid or salt of this nature. Because they were attempting to make their results comparable to those of some other investigator they arbitrarily chose a chromic acid concentration of 14.28 per cent.

III. Sargent found the optimum concentrations of bath constituents and the plating conditions for good deposits.

Most modern baths when subjected to a chemical analysis will prove to be almost identical to a Sargent bath in every essential respect. Subsequent work has modified, amplified and explained the conclusions of Carveth and Curry and of Sargent. The work of Haring and Barrows has been especially instrumental in pointing out the plating conditions consistent with best commercial practice of today. For example, in modern plating processes somewhat lower current densities are used and lower yields are obtained because it has been found more economical to do so. It is cheaper in America to plate a bright deposit at a low current efficiency than to plate a dull deposit with a higher current efficiency and pay for buffing.

The reasons for the slow development of commercial chromium plating in view of the excellent scientific research on plating baths has been due to several factors. There have been confusing and misleading statements published in the literature, materials of satisfactory purity have been commercially available for but a short time, and methods for analysis of chromic-acid baths require more study. Also, the necessity for control of plating conditions is much greater than for most other metals.

In the last few years, however, these obstructing factors have rapidly been reduced and it is not impossible that the next few years will bring simple and satisfactory methods of control, chemicals of greater purity, and a wider understanding of the principles underlying chromium deposition from chromic acid baths.

A summary of the historical development of chromium plating is presented in Appendix A, pages 122 to 126. The column headings are self-explanatory and require no further comment.

PART IV

BIBLIOGRAPHY

PART IV.

BIBLIOGRAPHY

1. 1852—C. J. E. Junot.
    Improvements in the Mode of Reducing Several Metallic Substances, and Applying Them, by Means of Electricity.
    B. P. 1183 (1853)
    Along with discussions on electrodepositing other metals, chromium is described as being capable of electrodeposition from the following solution: "I use chromium dissolved in a double chloride of soda and ammonia in the proportion of about 100 grams of metal to one kilogram of the salt dissolved in 10 liters of water." The temperature recommended is 30° to 40°C. with the use of platinum anodes.

2. 1854—R. Bunsen.
    Chromium Plating.
    Pogg. Ann. 91: 119. Also The Chemist. 11: 686.
    Chromium was deposited from a two-compartment cell; the anode was a carbon cell containing the acid; the cathode chamber contained the chromium solution and a platinum cathode.
    The electrolyte was a solution of chromous chloride containing some chromic salt.
    See p. 78 for further discussion.

3. 1856—A. Geuther.
    Electrolysis of Chromic Acid.
    Liebig. Ann. 99: 314.
    Electrolysis of 5%, 10%, 16% solutions of chromic acid, prepared by $K_2Cr_2O_7$ and H_2SO_4, gave metallic chromium, hydrogen, oxygen, and trivalent chromium. Complete data as to anode, current, voltage, hydrogen and chromium formed, etc., are given.

4. 1857—H. Buff.
    On the Behavior of Chromic Acid Under the Influence of the Electric Current.
    Liebig. Ann. 101: 1.
    Buff carefully repeated the work of Geuther. With pure chromic acid he did not obtain any metallic chromium at the cathode. He suggested reasons for some of the errors found in Geuther's results.

5. 1872—E. Ludwig.
    The Action of Chromic Acid on CO, H_2O, CH_4 and C_2H_4.
    Liebig. Ann. 162: 47.
    Saturated solutions of CrO_3 and even saturated solutions diluted down to 1:2 are reduced by CO in several hours. Only very concentrated solutions of CrO_3 act upon H_2. Methane is not attacked by CrO_3 in the least. Ethylene is oxidized by CrO_3 solutions.

6. 1878—A. Gawalovski.
    On the Storage of Chromic Acid.
    Zeit. analyt. Chemie. 17: 179–181.
    Gawalovski found that the purer the chromic acid the more difficult it was to reduce it with ordinary reagents such as alcohol. Even traces of sulphates greatly increase reactivity of CrO_3 solutions.

7. 1878—Morges.
    Thermal Researches on Chromates.
    Comp. Rend. 87: 15.
    Two lines of research are described: a study of the mode of decomposition of chromates; and a determination of the quantities of heat involved in these phenomena.
    In dilute solutions, electrolysis of chromic acid causes an evolution of oxygen and re-formation of chromic acid at the positive pole. In the negative compartment there is an evolution of hydrogen and formation of chromium chromate.

8. 1881—Alex. Classen.
    Electrolytic Determinations and Separations.
    Berichte der Deutschen Chemischen Gesellschafft. 14: 2777–2778.
    Methods are given for the electrolytic separation of chromium from iron and other metals.

9. 1883—A. Bartoli and G. Papasogli.
    Researches on Electrolyses with Carbon Electrodes of Solutions of Binary Composition and of Other Various Acids and Salts.
    Gazz. chim. Ital. 13: 47.
    "The negative electrode of carbon, employed in electrolyzing a solution of chromic acid, was found covered with a sheath of metallic chromium, most tenacious, most brilliant, (tenacissimo, splendidissimo), not attacked by air or water and which was deposited from chromium chromate formed during electrolysis."

10. 1884—T. Slater.
    Improvements in Electroplating Chromium Alloys.
    B. P. 5245.
    A method is given for electroplating alloys of chromium with other metals such as platinum, gold, nickel, copper, etc.

11. 1892—E. Placet.
     The Manufacture of Metallic Chromium by Electrolysis.
     Comptes rendus. 115: 945.
     A description of some electrodeposited chromium specimens is given.

12. 1894—E. Placet and J. Bonnet.
     Methods for Electrodepositing Chromium.
     U. S. P. 526114 (1894)
     Brit. P. 19344 (1891)
     Swed. P. 4257 (1893)
     D. R. P. 66099 (1892)
     Brit. P. 22854 (1892)
     Swed. P. 5863 (1895)
     Brit. P. 22855 (1892)
     Brit. P. (1892)
     Methods are described for depositing metallic chromium from chromic salts, chromic acid, and fuzed salt baths. See pp. 79 to 80 for a more complete discussion.

13. 1896—R. Whitney.
     Investigations on Chromium Sulphate Compounds.
     Zeit. f. physik. Chemie. 20: 40.
     A careful study was made of various chromic sulphate types. Various modifications showed different properties. A form $x(Cr_2(SO_4)_3, H_2SO_4)$ is described as a colloid.

14. 1898—Pascal Marino.
     Electrolytic Bath.
     U. S. P. 607646.
     A solution of chromium chloride is used containing some calcium sulphate.

15. 1896—J. A. W. Borchers.
     Electrometallurgy (Book).
     Page 366.
     The writer states that Bunsen's method for obtaining chromium has proven very satisfactory as a laboratory experiment.

16. 1899—J. F. L. Moeller and E. A. G. Street.
     Chromium Plating.
     Brit. Pat. 18743. D. R. P. 105847.
     Essentially a process of electrodepositing chromium from a solution of its sulphate.

17. 1898—J. W. Hittorf.
>   The Electromotive Behavior of Chromium.
>   Zeitschrift für Elektrochemie. 4: 482–492.
>
>   Cr was found electronegative to Zn, Cd, Fe, Ni, Cu, Hg, and Ag. Many tests were made using chromium as an anode in solutions of different substances and observing its behavior.
>
>   In the passive state Cr acts as a noble metal. If it is in a state where compounds of lowest valence are formed, it will deposit metals below zinc from solutions of their salts. There is a third state where chromium acts in a manner midway between the two above mentioned ways.

18. 1899—Boehringer and Sons.
>   Electrodeposition of Chromium.
>   D. R. P. 115463.
>
>   In this process a catholyte is used containing 500 g. of chromic sulphate, 500 g. of water, and 250 g. of sulphuric acid.

19. 1899—J. W. Hittorf.
>   The Behavior of Chromium.
>   Zeit. f. Electrochemie. 6: 6.
>
>   Passivity of chromium can not be explained by the formation of a thin oxide film over the metal.

20. 1899—C. L. Reese.
>   Electrolysis of Chromic Acid.
>   Action of Chromic Acid on Hydrogen Ion.
>   American Chemical Journal. 22: 158.
>
>   Chromic acid absorbed in clay, gypsum, etc., and placed in an atmosphere of hydrogen, was reduced in presence of platinized asbestos. H_2SO_4 hastened the process. Pure CrO_3 and pure H_2 even in presence H_2SO_4 did not interact.
>
>   Pure CrO_3 having no SO_4 was not reduced after a 24-hour electrolysis. A trace of SO_4 caused reduction to take place immediately. There is a limiting degree of reduction after which unlimited electrolysis will no longer reduce CrO_3. It seems there is a relationship between the limiting amount of reduction and the SO_4 concentration.

21. 1900—W. Ostwald.
>   On the Periodic Phenomena when Chromium is Dissolved in Acid.
>   Zeit. Phys. Chem. 35: 204–256.
>
>   A full discussion on the periodic active and passive states of chromium when dissolving in acids.

22. 1900—S. O. Cowper-Coles.
    Chromium Plating.
    Chemical News. 81: 16.

    Chromium is given a hardness of 7 as compared with nickel electroplate as 10 and cadmium plate as 4.5. The writer tried out Placet and Bonnet's solution with poor results. Good plate was obtained using a bath containing 75 parts water and 25 parts chromium chloride at 190°F. and 40–50 amperes per square foot. Hydrochloric acid had to be added to prevent excessive gassing. Lead anodes were used.

    The metal was found to have a good reflecting power and to be resistant to tarnish.

23. 1900—J. W. Hittorf.
    On the Passivity of Metals.
    Zeit. f. Elektrochemie. 7: 168.

24. 1900—H. Goldschmidt.
    Commercial Applications of Chromium Plate.
    Chem. News. 81: 17.
    Zeitschrift für Elektrochemie. 7: 668. (1901)
    Jahrbuch der Elektrochemie. 3: 233. (1901)

25. 1901—J. Férée.
    Electrolytic Chromium.
    Bull. Soc. Chim. (3) 25: 617.

    The writer obtained steel-gray chromium, 99.82% pure, by using a Pt cathode and electrolyzing a solution of 740 g. H_2O, 100 g. HCl, and 160 g. crystallized $CrCl_3$, CD = 0.15 amp. per cm²., 8 volts.

    A better bath contained 266.5 g. $CrCl_3 \cdot 6H_2O$ and 223.58 KCl in 1 l. H_2O.

    The current efficiency was 45%. A diaphragm was used.

    For further details see page 81.

26. 1901—B. Neumann.
    Account of G. Glaser's Experiments on Chromium Plating.
    Zeit. f. Elektrochemie. 7: 656.

    This is an account of Glaser's experiments in depositing chromium. In a two-cell apparatus he used solutions of chromic chloride, chromic sulphate, and chromic acetate, respectively, as the catholyte. The anolyte consisted of mineral acid or salt solutions. The best current efficiency proved to be about 85%. Sulphates and chlorides proved satisfactory; acetate solutions gave low yields.

27. 1901—Erich Müller.
   On Disturbances of Cathodic Depolarization by Means of Potassium Chromate.
   Zeit. f. Elektrochemie. 7: 398–405.
   A discussion of the function of K_2CrO_4 in electrolytic hypochlorite cells.

28. 1901—R. Luther.
   Single Potentials of Chromium.
   Zeit. Phys. Chem. 36: 389.
   Luther found the single potentials of chromium to be
   0.3 volt against divalent salts
   0.2 volt against trivalent salts and
   −0.9 volt against hexavalent salts.
   These figures assume a value of −0.56 volt for the Ostwald normal electrode.

29. 1902—Erich Müller.
   An addition to article referred to in 27.
   Zeit. f. Elektrochemie. 8: 909–915.

30. 1904—M. Le Blanc.
   The Production of Chromium and Its Compounds by the Aid of Electric Current.
   Book pp. 1–32.
   A monograph on the subject of the electrolytic production of chromium. In the part devoted to electrolysis of aqueous solutions, the writer discusses in detail the different patent claims to date. He singles out Placet and Bonnet and expresses doubts as to their veracity. A summary of various good trivalent chromium salt baths is given.

31. 1905—H. R. Carveth and W. R. Mott.
   Electrolytic Chromium I.
   Jour. Phys. Chem. 9: 231–256.
   Chromium was deposited from solutions of trivalent salts of chromium. A two-compartment cell and platinum electrodes were used. In the cathode cell part of the trivalent salt was reduced and deposition actually took place from a divalent ion. A discussion is given of the work of earlier investigators.
   This article is given more discussion on pages 81 to 82.

32. 1905—H. R. Carveth and B. E. Curry.
   Electrolytic Chromium II.
   Jour. Phys. Chem. 9: 353–380.
   Reprinted Trans. Am. Electrochem. Soc. 7: 115ff.
   Chromium can be deposited from solutions of chromic acid in the presence of an impurity such as sulphuric acid. Many solutions are dis-

cussed along with a treatment of the work of earlier investigators. Detailed discussion is given on pages 83 to 85.

In the discussion following the presentation of the paper at the American Electrochemical Society deposits are described which did not flake off even when the plated piece was severely distorted.

33. 1906—O. Dony-Henault.
    Zeit. f. Elektrochemie. 12: 329.

The modification, green or violet, in which Cr''' exists is an important factor in the electrodeposition process. The violet form is much more favorable to deposition.

34. 1906—M. Le Blanc.
    Chromium Plating.
    Trans. Am. Electrochem. Soc. 9: 315–327.

Paper deals with controversy about depositing chromium electrolytically. A good deposit can be obtained on copper, brass, or carbon, but the coating is very thin, in this case, 0.13 mm. thick. A thicker deposit tends to peel off. Chromium sulphate was used as electrolyte with a lead anode and copper cathode.

35. 1906—
    Discussion following the presentation of the previous paper.
    Trans. Am. Electrochem. Soc. 9: 327–328.

Pres. Bancroft: I call attention again to the samples of chromium which were shown at Boston last year, and must express a certain regret that Le Blanc should not have put more time on the question of depositing chromium from chromic acid. The work with chromium sulphate and chromium chloride showed that only under great precautions could one get a satisfactory deposit of chromium. The real solution from which to deposit chromium is not chrome alum nor chromium sulphate, it is chromic acid. When you were inspecting the laboratory the other day we made some chromium before your eyes. I cannot believe that it is impossible to plate that chromium to any desired thickness. If the solutions remain unchanged and the conditions remain unchanged you are bound to get the deposit to any thickness you please. That has been shown perfectly satisfactorily in regard to nickel. People make statements that you cannot precipitate nickel to more than infinitesimal thickness. You cannot if you do not keep the conditions constant. You can deposit to any thickness you please, and a chromic acid solution is an ideal one in which to keep the bath perfectly constant. So far as I know, no one here has ever plated chromium to the thickness of one inch, but I feel certain that it is merely a question of power to do it. If there is any real inducement to plate chromium an inch thick, we will do it.

Mr. Curry: We ran some few plates and made long runs, and we had chromium deposits that were very good. They were more than a millimeter in thickness, which is more than six times as thick as Prof. Le Blanc says that he could plate. We did not make but two or three of those deposits; but so far as we tried it we were very successful.

Mr. Carveth: In all the experiments which Mr. Curry and myself have made with chromic acid, to get good platings, we used a single compartment cell. The electrolyte was delivered at the cathode, went over the cathode around over the anode, and made a continuous circulation. You might then have a far better chance of obtaining thicker deposits.

36. 1907—F. Salzer.

   Process for Producing an Electrolytic Deposit of Metallic Chromium.
   D. R. P. 221472 (1910)

   Chromium is deposited from a bath containing CrO_3 and Cr_2O_3 in a ratio of 2:1. Small amounts of sulphuric acid are beneficial. More discussion is given on pages 87 to 88.

37. 1909—F. Salzer.

   Process for Obtaining Galvanic Chromium Deposits.
   D. R. P. 225769 (1910)

   This is an addition to Salzer's earlier patent (see 36). A solution of the following composition is described:

CrO_3	13%
Cr_2O_3	11%
$Cr_2(SO_4)_3$	12%
Remainder water.	

38. 1910—J. Voisin.

   Electrolytic Chromium.
   Revue de Metallurgie. 7: 1137–1148.

   There is given an account of a careful investigation of the work of Placet and Bonnet, Möller and Street, Cowper-Coles, Férée, and Carveth and Mott. Solutions of chloride, fluoride, and sulphate of chromium were used. The effect of boric acid was investigated.

39. 1910—Hans Kuessner.

   The Anodic Behavior of Molybdenum, Manganese, Chromium and Tantalum.
   Zeit. f. Elektrochem. 16: 754–772.

   Anodic reactions have been very carefully worked out. The average valency of solution varies with current density in the case of chromium.

40. 1911—F. Flade.
    Contributions to the Knowledge of Passivity.
    Z. Physik. Chem. 76: 513–46.

    A discussion of work done on the passivity of iron, nickel, and chromium. The writer finds nothing to substantiate the oxide theory with respect to chromium.

41. 1912—M. Baum.
    A Method for the Production of Filament Holders for Metal Filament Electric Incandescent Lamps.
    B. P. 16865 (1913).

    A method is described whereby a nickel wire is coated with chromium by electrodeposition in a bath "which consists of a 10-per-cent solution of chromic acid to which from 0.5 to 1.0 per cent of a suitable acid, for example, boric acid or tartaric acid or the like is added." Where low current densities are used a bath is described as containing essentially 10 per cent of chromic acid and 10 per cent of chromium sulphate to which boric acid may optionally be added.

    "If this operation is carried out within determined limits of current deposits varying from pure metal to chromous hydroxide, $Cr(OH)_2$, are obtained. . . . ."

42. 1913—P. Askenasy and A. Revai.
    On the Electrolytic Regeneration of Chromic Acid from Chromic Sulphate Solutions.
    Zeit. f. Electrochemie. 19: 344–362.

    The paper gives the best conditions whereby chromic acid is regenerated from chromic sulphate solutions without use of diaphragms. In an appendix the authors discuss chromium plating literature and state that they have been able to confirm Carveth and Curry's conclusions that chromium can be deposited from a chromic acid solution only if a small amount of sulphate impurity is present.

43. 1918—A. H. W. Aten.
    The Passivity of Chromium.
    Proc. Acad. Sci. Amsterdam. 20: 812–823.

    A review of theories of passivity is given. Cr metal for electrodes was made by electrolyzing a solution containing 13% CrO_3 and 12% $Cr_2(SO_4)_3$. The cathode was rotated at 800 r.p.m. and by using a current density of 80 amp./dcm^2; a 15% yield was obtained.

    Potential of Cr against $Cr_2(SO_4)_3$ proved to be -0.75 volts or -0.47 volts, referred to H.

44. 1920—G. J. Sargent.
    Electrolytic Chromium.
    Trans. Am. Electrochem. Soc. 37: 479–496.

    Sargent has determined the effects of cathode stirring, changing CrO_3 and $Cr_2(SO_4)_3$ concentrations, temperature and current density on the yield of metallic chromium.

    A deposit 1.15 cm. thick was deposited from a bath containing 25% CrO_3 and 0.3% $Cr_2(SO_4)_3$ at 10 amp. per square decimeter at 20°C.

    More discussion is given on pages 85 to 87.

45. 1921—E. Liebreich.
    Causes of the Periodic Phenomena in the Electrolysis of Chromic Acid and the Deposition of Metallic Chromium.
    Zeit. f. Elektrochemie. 27: 94–110. 27: 452.
    Also D. R. P. 398054 (Applied for 1920, granted 1924).

    The electrolysis of aqueous solutions of H_2CrO_4 between platinum electrodes has been investigated at 20°C. It has been found that the decomposition voltage curve consists of a system of 4 curves which lie close to one another and which run together at low current densities and voltages; and that at certain current densities the voltage passes abruptly from one curve to another. The periodic phenomena observed during the electrolysis of H_2CrO_4 are due to the repetition of these abrupt voltage changes. Each of the curves which branch off from the main curves is a deposition curve of a definite chromium compound. The curve lying nearest to the voltage and farthest from the current density coördinate is the deposition curve for metallic chromium. The periodic phenomena in the electrolysis of H_2CrO_4 are manifested when there occur an alternate reduction and reoxidation of the deposited product; they are not passivity phenomena. It has not been found possible to deposit metallic chromium with current densities above 0.45 amperes per square centimeter (20°C.). The deposits of chromium with small current densities have a bright metallic appearance and adhere with great tenacity.

46. 1921—E. Liebreich.
    Influence of Chlorides on the Decomposition Voltage Curves of Chromic Acid.
    Zeit. f. Elektrochemie. 27: 452–455.

    The chromic oxides or hydroxides observed in deposition of chromium from CrO_3 are colloidal in nature. Chlorides in the bath cause displacement of the decomposition voltage-current density curves.

47. 1921—E. Liebreich.
Process for Electrolytic Deposition of Metallic Chromium.
D. R. P. 406665.

The reduction of chromic acid to the lower oxides of chromium, which, although it is not so stated, is only a partial reduction, is accomplished by heating chromic acid having a sulphuric acid content of less than 1.2 per cent in the absence of air to from 170°C. to 200°C.

48. 1921—G. Grube.
Process for the Electrolytic Deposition of Pure Chromium in Thick Layers.
Swiss P. 103928, also U. S. P. 1496845 (1924).

The plating bath consists essentially of the following: 1. A concentrated solution of chromic acid to which a small amount of a "foreign" acid such as sulphuric is added. To this, chromoxide is added in such proportions that there is an excess of chromoxide after it has neutralized the "foreign acid."

2. The ratio of chromic acid to chromoxide must be greater than 2:1.

3. This relationship must be maintained within narrow limits during electrolysis. For example, a solution containing 250 g./l. CrO_3, 3 g./l. $Cr_2(SO_4)_3$ maintains approximately that ratio if proper CrO_3 additions are made from time to time.

Another claim is that in choosing the current densities at anode and cathode the above ratio is maintained.

49. 1922—Spiro Kyropoulos.
Metallographic Investigations of the Cathodic Separation of Metals on Al and Cr.
Zeit. f. Anorg. und All. Chemie. 119: 299–304.
J. Inst. Metals. 29: 669.

Aluminum and chromium were investigated as cathode materials. Copper deposited from copper ammonium chloride, and silver from silver nitrate deposited only on the crystal boundaries of the aluminum. Very few crystal nuclei deposited upon the face of aluminum crystals. Cyanide baths were much better; the metal had a greater tendency to deposit on crystal faces. In fact any plating process wherein H_2 is discharged along with metal acts this way.

Using chromium as a cathode it was found that silver nitrate deposited silver only at the crystal boundaries if the chromium was passive. The treatment of the chromium was as follows: etched in HCl and passified in HNO_3. Upon activating the chromium cathodically, both copper and silver deposited much more evenly. Cyanide baths acted relatively the same as in the case of aluminum.

Passive nickel behaved the same as aluminum and passive chromium when used as cathode.

50. 1922—W. E. Hughes.
　　　Chromium Plating.
　　　Modern Electroplating (book) p. 138.
　　　A deposit of chromium is described which was so soft that it was capable of being scratched with the thumb nail.

51. 1922—E. Liebreich.
　　　Chromium Electroplating.
　　　Zeit. f. Metallkunde. 14: 367–368.
　　　Repetition of a former article. Good plate was obtained at current densities of 10–85 amperes per square decimeter and voltages of 2.2 to 3.6. Dull deposits were obtained when the yield was 50%; bright plate at 25%. Liebreich gives some corrosion data.

52. 1922—E. Macqueron.
　　　Determination of Chromium and Iron in Commercial Solutions of Chromium Salts.
　　　Rev. Prod. Chim. 25: 799–800.
　　　The chromium is oxidized in alkaline solution with Na_2O_2, the $Fe(OH)_3$ is filtered off. Fe and Cr are determined by $KMnO_4$ titration.

53. 1923—K. W. Schwartz.
　　　Chromium Plating Steel Using Chromium Anodes.
　　　Trans. Am. Electrochem. Soc. 44: 451–463.
　　　Metal Industry. 21: 441.
　　　A series of runs were made electrolyzing a Sargent bath between chromium anodes. Best results were obtained at current densities of 9.3–16 amperes per square decimeter. No beneficial results were obtained by heating or stirring the bath. No plate was obtained without a simultaneous evolution of hydrogen at the cathode. Chromium anodes were used and no passivity was noted. Chrome-plated steel resists corrosive attacks of air saturated with NH_3, HNO_3, or H_2O. It is not attacked by molten Sn, Zn, or brass.

54. 1923—Colin G. Fink.
　　　Chromium Plating.
　　　Brass World. 19: 328.
　　　Note on high current density required. Believes high evolution of hydrogen gas at the cathode serves as a protection for the chromium.

55. 1923—Colin G. Fink.
　　　The Color of Chromium.
　　　Brass World. 19: 322.
　　　The color of chromium is silver white. It is the only metal that will stay bright in a laboratory atmosphere. Not even platinum will stay as bright.

56. 1923—A. Thiel and W. Hammerschmidt.
    The Relation Between Hydrogen Overvoltage on Pure Metals and Certain Properties of the Metals.
    Zeit. f. Anorg. und Allgemeine Chemie. 132: 15–35.
    A very complete table of overvoltages is given.

57. 1923—E. Liebreich.
    Chromium Plating Process.
    Metal Industry. 21: 488.

58. 1923—N. Isgarishev and A. Obrutsheva.
    The Behavior of Chromium During Electrolysis with Alternating Currents.
    Zeit. f. Elektrochemie. 29: 428–434.
    The solubility of chromium as electrodes was determined in H_2SO_4, KOH, and KCl under simultaneous use of direct and alternating currents. The latter increased the solubility evidently breaking down the colloidal skin. Cr went into solution as Cr''' and Cr^{VI} in varying proportions.
    In an H_2SO_4 solution chromium dissolves principally as Cr''' with the passage of alternating current. Some Cr^{VI} is formed.
    The passage of direct current dissolves chromium as Cr^{VI}.
    The above tests were repeated using a KOH bath. No results were obtained due to the formation of a hydroxide skin on the metal.
    N/1 HCl formed relatively more Cr^{VI} than Cr''' than a solution containing H_2SO_4.
    Passivity of chromium is explained by a colloidal oxide skin.

59. 1923—G. C. Schmidt.
    On Passivity.
    Zeit. Phys. Chemie. 106: 147.

60. 1923—E. Liebreich.
    Electrodeposition of Chromium.
    Z. Electrochemie. 24: 208.
    J. Inst. Met. 30: 616.

61. 1923—E. Liebreich.
    Electrodeposition of Chromium.
    Zeit. f. Elektrochemie. 29: 208–210.
    It is concluded that in the chromic acid process chromium is deposited from a divalent ion.

62. 1923—F. Auerbach.
    The Constitution of Aqueous Chromic Acid Solutions.
    Zeit. Anorg. Allgem. Chem. 126: 54.
    The first dissociation constant of H_2CrO_4 is great; the second is small.

63. 1923—Erik Liebreich.
    Electrolytic Chromium Deposition.
    Zeit. f. Elektrochemie. 29: 208–210.
    Jour. Inst. Met. 30: 616.

    Liebreich reiterates his statements that the current density-decomposition voltage curve of H_2CrO_4 consists of 4 branches. His baths consisted of 22 g. CrO_3, 1.78 g. H_2SO_4, and 100 cc. water; 22 g. CrO_3, .009 g. H_2SO_4, and 100 cc. water and were run at different temperatures.

    Metal deposition is a matter of reducing Cr^{++} from the hydroxide film at the cathode.

64. 1923—A. Kleffner.
    Periodic Phenomena in the Electrolysis of Chromic Acid.
    Zeit. f. Elektrochemie. 29: 488–491.

    Quotes unpublished work of Miss Collenberg that no periodicity takes place in absence of SO_4.

    Pure Kahlbaum CrO_3 gave but one slight hump in the current density-decomposition voltage curve.

    Mercks CrO_3 contained H_2SO_4 and gave a curve similar to Liebreich's. He believes, however, that some of the breaks in the curve are not due to new compounds but to other factors. Platinum and iron cathodes were used.

    Work was done with 440 g./l. CrO_3 and with varying amounts of H_2SO_4 up to 100% of N/10 H_2SO_4.

    On Cr cathodes there were no breaks in the current density-cathode potential curve with pure CrO_3. With H_2SO_4 added the behavior was the same as on Pt and Fe, that is, one break was noted.

    Some breaks in the curve occur when Cr is first deposited on a foreign metal. On Cr or on a Cr-plated piece this break is eliminated.

65. 1923—K. Oyabu.
    A Contribution on the Electrical Precipitation of Chromium.
    Zeit. f. Elektrochemie. 29: 491–493.

    Writer gets only one break in the current density-decomposition voltage curve, checks Sargent (see 44) and disagrees with Liebreich (see 45). Experiments show that the form of the curve depends on the nature of the cathode material.

66. 1923—H. Wolff.
    Electrolytic Deposition of Chromium.
    D. R. P. 422461. (1925).

    A process is given for the manufacture of chromium anodes by means of pressing and sintering powdered chromium. Iron anodes are described.

67. 1923—Spiro Kyropoulos.
Coating Iron and Iron Alleys with Chromium.
U. S. P. 1590101 (1926).

This patent deals with the formation of what is practically a layer of stainless steel on the surface of steel. If a piece of steel is chromium plated and then heated to such a temperature as to cause diffusion at the metal interface, often the adherence of the outer coating is poor. This is especially true if the carbon content of the steel is high.

In order to obtain good adherence it is decided to have an intermediary layer of carbon-free metal such as electrodeposited iron or other metal between the steel and the chromium plate. The material is then heated in a non-oxidizing atmosphere to from 1000°C. to 1300°C. and an iron-chromium alloy forms which has many of the properties of stainless steel.

68. 1923—A. J. Coignard.
Obtaining Chromium by Electrolysis.
Fr. P. 571447. (1924).

The use of ferro-chrome anodes is described and their advantages given over lead anodes. Due to the fragility of ferro-chrome such anodes are best supported by grids or bands or by other holders made of lead.

By varying the current density an alloy of iron and chromium can be obtained.

The chromium-plating bath may be acid, neutral, or basic. It may be made of chromic chloride or other salt; bichromate of soda or chromic acid.

69. 1923—R. E. Search.
Anodes for Chromium Plating.
Metal Industry. 21: 272.

The author tells where lead anodes for chromium plating can be procured.

70. 1923—R. E. Search.
Chromium Plating.
Metal Industry. 21: 109.

The special properties of chromium arise from the fact that it shows a potential equivalent almost equal to that of the noble metals, and chemically it is as resistant to oxidation under certain conditions.

For years electrochemists have tried to find a way of depositing chromium in an adhesive state upon other metals. Bunsen was the first to successfully deposit chromium. He did his work in 1850. It was not until after many years of research that it was discovered that during the electrolysis of chromic acid and other chromium salts, there took place a gradual reduction of the chromic to chromous salts. This was the key to the process.

Chromium in its electrolytic deposition is much inclined to exfoliation and also occlude hydrogen within its pores. Nevertheless, dense and adherent, but thin, coatings may be obtained, if, along with the chromium salt, there is added chromic acid to the electrolyte. By this means, the overloading of the hydrogen will be reduced and the exfoliation of the chromium will be prevented.

The deposit of chromium upon copper, brass and nickel is compact, hard and adherent. Depending upon the condition of the electrolyte, the physical appearance changes from that of a gray powder to a mirror-clear luster. With the gray powdered deposit a fast, adhering coat, at least one millimeter thick can be obtained, while with the lustrous deposit the thickness reaches only one-tenth of a millimeter.

The current density for depositing chromium varies from five to ten amperes per square decimeter and is five to ten times higher than what is required for depositing nickel.

In the Berlin Städtische Gas Works, the large gas main in front of the cyanide washer was chromium plated. After two months of service it had not been affected by its severe trial.

If a solution containing 12% $Cr(SO_4)_3$, 13% CrO_3, and 11% Cr_2O_3 is taken, a good deposit of chromium may be obtained on the cathode if lead dioxide anodes are used. The principal difficulty in this process is the preparation of the anodes. For sulphuric acid solutions, anodes coated over with lead dioxide may be used.

71. 1924—G. Grube and H. Burkhart.
    Chromium Plated Cathodes.
    Chem. and Met. Eng. 30: 639.
    Ind. Eng. Chem. 16: 537.

    In laboratory experiments, it was possible to obtain pure solutions of hypochlorites and chlorates without addition of substances to prevent reduction. This was accomplished by using Cr-plated cathodes.

72. 1924—E. Liebreich and W. Wiederholt.
    Passivity Phenomena and Cathodic Over-Voltage.
    Zeit. f. Elektrochemie. 30: 263–279.

    1. From the current-voltage curve of chromium it follows that it is easily made passive; if the chemical conditions in its surroundings are such that trivalent Cr oxide may be formed.

    2. The passivity of Cr is probably accounted for by the insolubility of this oxide.

    3. The passivity of Fe is distinguished from that of Cr principally through the fact that it originates in the highest degree of oxidation of iron.

    4. Chromium and iron became activated at lower cathode polarization during hydroxide formation. This activation period depends on the concentration of hydroxide ions in the neighborhood of the cathode.

5. It appears possible that the overvoltage for the cathodic separation of metals finds its explanation likewise in the alloying property of the metal instead of the H with the cathode material.

73. 1924—P. Winkler, J. Sigrist, and M. Wantz.
    Obtaining Chromium by Electrolytic Methods.
    Chem. and Met. Eng. 31: 710ff.
    Arch. Sc. physc. et. nat. Geneve. (S) 6 Supp. 112–115.
    Chromium can be deposited from CrO_3 or from Cr^{+++} salt solution.
    1. A concentrated Sargent bath was used with following results:
    Mimimum voltage for deposition = 3.4 volts. Current efficiency at room temperature at 160 amp/sq.dcm. = .16–.17 g/amp. hour.
    The best, coherent deposit was obtained without heat but by a low current density.
    The state of the cathode surface, polish, is of great consequence.
    The time duration of the electrolysis is unimportant to the quality of the deposit.
    The presence of $Cr_2(SO_4)_3$ is indispensible.
    Ferric salts, $CaSO_4$, and Na_2SO_4, reduced the yield and deteriorated the quality of the plate.
    2. Chromium can be deposited from a Cr^{+++} salt solution if the concentration is kept up and a definite pH is maintained. In all cases, the yield and quality of deposit is inferior to that of a CrO_3 bath.

74. 1924—J. Sigrist, P. Winkler, and M. Wantz.
    Experiments in Obtaining Chromium Electrolytically.
    Helv. Chim. Acta. 7: 968–972.
    Same data are presented as 73.
    Additional information is given on the use of trivalent chromium salts. With the use of $CrCl_3$ or $Cr_2(SO_4)_3$ a diaphragm is necessary. If pH is too low, a hydroxide slime is deposited; if pH is too high, no plate is formed.

75. 1924—E. Liebreich.
    The Periodic Phenomena in the Electrolysis of Chromic Acid.
    Zeit. f. Elektrochemie. 30: 186–187.
    Answers to Kleffner and Oyabu (see 64 and 65). With addition of SO_4 to solutions of CrO_3, the three breaks in the cathode potential-current density curve tend to shift. Only in pure solutions are they distinct.

76. 1924—H. Gruber.
    Hydrogen Content of Electrodeposited Chromium.
    Zeit. f. Elektrochemie. 30. 396.
    Chromium deposited in thick layers is of such a nature that at low temperatures it begins to give off hydrogen. In boiling water, small quantities of hydrogen are given off which can be collected and identified.

The hydrogen in chromium appears to be in much looser combination than that in iron.

A sample of chromium plate 5 by 3 by 4 centimeters was heated in a Bunsen flame. The escape of hydrogen out of the metal was noticeable. Upon cutting off the gas supply from the burner, the hydrogen continued to burn on the surface of the metal. After 20 seconds, the hydrogen flame grew faint and finally was extinguished. The temperature of the metal was so low that no oxidation took place. The same experiments performed on iron known to contain much hydrogen, did not yield the same results.

77. 1924—E. Liebreich.
   On the Electrodeposition of Metallic Chromium.
   Met. Ind. (London) 450–54.

The electrodeposition of chromium metal has lately become very important on account of the special qualities of this metal. In order to obtain chromium metal by electrolysis, the presence of the bi-equivalent chromium is essential.

Attention must be drawn to the fact that a solution containing chromic acid entirely changes in its chemical components in a very short time through the effect of the electric current.

The baths to be used for chromium plating differ completely from the baths used for nickel plating.

While oxidation of a solution containing chromic acid hardly takes place because the oxygen completely escapes, or will form peroxides if lead anodes are used, the reduction on the cathode is, on the contrary, a very strong one, so that the electrolyte has soon changed completely. Apart from theoretical proof, this may be seen by the change of color of the solution. The bath, which at the beginning contained chromic acid has changed very quickly into a solution of oxides, and only small traces of pure chromic acid are noticeable. Similar conditions prevail in respect to baths in which components of chromium of the atomicity 3 are added, as these conditions are also altered by the electric current, and components are formed of tri- and bi-equivalent oxides of chromium. It is a mistake to believe that the bath would then still be of the composition as it was at first, and as some inventors presume. This different condition will also prevail when the current is switched off. This is the principal difference between the baths for chromium plating and the baths for plating usual metals as nickel or copper. This peculiarity of the Cr plating is naturally based on the multi-atomicity of Cr.

The conditions which must be observed for separating metallic chromium in the presence of oxides of mean atomicity down to atomicity of 2 are these. The more a bath has of such, and the more the other conditions are adjusted to fit them, the better the bath is working and the better it gives the yield.

In view of these facts, it seems to be suitable to warn against the conception that Cr plating is a process which can be used by any person, or that processes which are claimed to be original are quite without consideration of the fact that solutions of chromic acid are changed by the current.

78. 1924—Gillet.
    The Use of Chromium Plating in Electric Furnaces.
    Metal Industry. 22: 197.

79. 1924—C. B. Bellis.
    The Importance of Chromium to the Engineer.
    Chem. and Met. Vol. 30, p. 151.

    The most important uses of metallic chromium are in the manufacture of chromium wire and as an anode in chromium plating. Malleable wire is made as a result of the researches of E. R. Richardson. The wire is made by depositing chromium on copper wire, drawing down, replating, redrawing, and repeating these operations until the copper wire is of negligible cross section.

    Chromium which has been electrolytically deposited, though hard, is malleable, while ordinary metallic chromium is brittle. The principal reason for the brittleness is the very high temperature at which cast chromium has always been produced. Another reason is the presence of occluded gas and oxide.

    Chromium plating, while it is as yet hardly a commercial process, has now been done very successfully. A great current density is used and the large volume of H_2 evolved at the cathode provides the condition necessary to prevent the chromium from oxidizing again and passing back into solution.

    Chromium plating has been found to give protection in cases where other platings have failed. The chromium plate is hard and can not be buffed or polished. The ability of chromium-plated steel to resist corrosion even exceeds chromium alloys. One disadvantage of chromium alloys and chromium-plated objects is that they will not resist hydrochloric acid.

80. 1924—E. Maas.
    Protection of Metals.
    Z. Verein deut. Ing. 68: 880–883.

    A discussion of seven theories of corrosion with special reference to brass condenser tubes. Use of metallic and non-metallic coatings is reviewed. Cr and lithopone offer wide commercial applications.

81. 1925—C. G. Fink.
    Process of Electrodepositing Chromium and Preparing Baths Therefor.
    U. S. P. 1581188. (1926).

    There is given in the specifications a theoretical conception of chromium deposition from chromic-acid baths. It is claimed that chromium is reduced at the cathode, during electrolysis, behind a "protecting hydrogen film." However, a "catalyst" also is necessary, this "catalyst" being a stable acid radical, such as sulphate. Unstable radicals, such as the nitrate, may be used, but have to be replenished from time to time. Specifically the patent covers for a solution containing 250 grams per liter of chromic acid with the presence of 1 up to 5 grams of sulphate radical per liter. If the chromic acid concentration be increased, then the sulphate must also be changed accordingly. A chemically equivalent amount of another radical may be substituted.

It is pointed out that ordinary commercial chromic acid contains other acid radicals as impurities. Therefore, the amounts of sulphates or other radicals to be added should be so governed as to have the total sulphate or other radical content within the above described limits.

Although in the claims only the word catalyst appears, in the specifications suitable "catalysts" are defined as being "acids and bases having a sulphate radical; acids and bases having a fluoride radical; acids and bases having a phosphate radical; acids and bases having a borate radical."

In 1928 a disclaimer added to the patent disclaims processes in which regulation of the anion concentration is not practiced.

Temperatures are kept from 15°C. to 40°C. with current densities of from 36 to 144 amperes per square foot.

82. 1925—H. E. Haring.
Principles and Operating Conditions of Chromium Plating.
Chem. and Met. Eng. 32: 692, 756.

Procedure used at the Bureau of Printing and Engraving is given. The solution consists of 250 g./l. of CrO_3, 3 g./l. $Cr_2(SO_4)_3$, and 7 g./l. Cr carbonate. An operating chart is given in which the proper current density for any temperature can be found. Pb anodes are used.

83. 1925—A. E. Ollard.
Resistance to Corrosion of Electrodeposited Chromium.
Engineer. 140: 236.
Electrical Review. 97: 393.
Chem. Age. 13: 245.
Engineering. 120: 408.
Metal Ind. 23: 454.

Abridgements of paper discussed on pages 91 to 93. The corrosion resistance of iron objects plated with chromium and with various combinations of metals is compared.

84. 1925—A. E. Ollard.
Corrosion Resistance of Chromium Plated Iron.
Metal Industry (London). 27: 235–237.
Discussion to paper referred to on pages 91 to 93.

85. 1925—G. M. Enos.
    Notes on the Plating of Chromium on Steel.
    Trans. Am. Electrochem. Soc. 48: 37–44.

   Steel can be chromium plated by the methods described by Schwartz, but it is recommended that the temperature of the solution be kept low.

   For periods up to six hours, and temperatures up to 1,050°C., no combination of chromium plating, heat treating for diffusion, and case hardening could be found that would give surfaces which were hard, and at the same time in such physical shape as to make it likely that they would resist corrosive media. Chromium plate on steel prevents cementation for the ordinary time and temperature conditions employed in case hardening.

86. 1926—G. Grube, R. Heidinger, and L. Schlecht.
    The Electrochemical Behavior of Chromium.
    Zeit. f. Elektrochemie. 32: 70–79.

   1. At low current densities, chromium dissolves as Cr'' in H_2SO_4, HCl, NaCl, and KOH.

   2. Chromium undergoes a secondary reaction forming some chromates in solutions of H_2SO_4, HCl, cold NaCl, and KOH. In hot solutions of NaCl, Cr'' oxidizes to Cr'''; Cr^{VI} is formed only at very high current densities.

   3. In all cases the anode potential-current density curves of active chromium break into stages separated by one volt or more.

   4. In alkaline solutions, Cr becomes passive, probably due to a film of oxide.

87. 1926—D. T. Ewing and A. M. Malloy.
    The Electrolytic Deposition of Chromium.
    Michigan State College Bulletin #7 of the Engineering Experiment Station.

   This paper includes a number of references to original investigations on the preparation of electrolytic chromium which made it especially adaptable for hardness and the protection of iron and steel against atmospheric corrosion. The base metal may or may not be plated with copper or nickel when hardness is especially desired. A comparative study is made of several standard chromic acid baths, and also the effect of the addition of various substances to solutions of chromic acid. Finally, several new baths are described, with a small amount of mercury, or salts of mercury as an addition agent. The original cost of installing a chromium plating equipment is not high and the cost of operation is low. The greatest cost is in the preparation of the surface preparatory to plating.

88. 1926—E. Liebreich.
    Chromium Plating.
    Met. Ind. u. Gal. Tech. 24: 7.

89. 1926—P. W. C. Strausser.
>   Chromium Plating Progress.
>   Metal Industry. 24: 372ff.
>
>   A large amount of data are given of the behavior at various current densities and temperatures of a solution containing 200 g./l. CrO_3, 5 g./l. $Cr_2(SO_4)_3$ and 3 g./l. H_3BO_3. Other solutions are mentioned. There is a discussion of uses for chromium plate.

90. 1926—A. E. Ollard.
>   General Survey of Chromium Plating.
>   Metal Industry. 24: 110.

91. 1926—A. Butziger.
>   Chromium Plating in the German Pressed-glass Industry.
>   Metallwaren-Ind. Galvano-Tech. 24: 267–268.
>
>   Details of the plant of Glassfabrik A. G. Brockwitz for Cr-plating cast-iron glass-molds are shown and this use of Cr plating is discussed.

92. 1926—E. Kruppa.
>   Removing the Lead Danger in Chromium-Plating Plants.
>   Metallwaren-Ind. Galvano-Tech. 24: 310–311.
>
>   The danger of Pb poisoning is avoided by substituting other materials for Pb. Stoneware tanks and suction ducts are used, Al heating and cooling coils, and a special Al alloy has been developed for use as an anode which does not dissolve appreciably and yet permits sufficient current to flow for plating.

93. 1926—E. Kruppa.
>   New Ways for Removing the Injurious Fumes of Electroplating Baths, Especially Chromium-Plating Baths.
>   Metallwaren-Ind. Galvano-Tech. 24: 408–409.
>
>   The complicated exhausting equipment and loss of electrolyte can be avoided by covering the surface of the bath with a layer of material which is unaffected by the bath such as paraffin oil, cork particles coated with paraffin or glass wool soaked in paraffin, etc. The gases evolved do not carry any electrolyte with them after being forced to diffuse through this surface layer.

94. 1926—E. Müller.
>   Theory of the Electrolytic Separation of Chromium From Aqueous Chromic-acid Solutions.
>   Zeit. f. Elektrochemie. 32: 399–413.
>
>   A number of cathode current density-cathode potential curves of C, Pt, Hg (also Cu, Pd, and Au) in solutions of specially purified CrO_3 and CrO_3 to which H_2SO_4 and Na_2SO_4 were added. The curves are explained and correlated on the basis of the assumption of a diaphragm or film of Cr_2O_3 or

$Cr_2(CrO_4)_3$ on the cathode. No direct evidence could be found for the existence of such a diaphragm in the electrolysis of pure CrO_3 aside from the course of the I-V curves but its existence is assumed, and Müller considers that this diaphragm prevents access of unreduced CrO_3 to the cathode and no reduction takes place. In the presence of SO_4 this diaphragm is damaged and reduction takes place. Other anions behave similarly as was found by adding NaCl, $NaNO_3$, $NaClO_3$, and $NaSiF_6$ to pure CrO_3. H_3PO_4 has no effect nor do CrO_4 ions have the effect of SO_4 ions as was found by adding Na or Ca chromate. Pure CrO_3 gave only a blackish powdery appearing deposit of Cr but a white and under certain conditions bright deposit was obtained when SO_4 and other anions were added. $Cr_2(SO_4)_3$ and H_2SO_4 in equivalent amounts have the same action as Na_2SO_4. Many details of theory are discussed.

95. 1926—W. Pfanhauser.
     The Process of Chromium Plating (Das Verchromungs-Verfahren).
     Press of the Langbein Pfanhauser Werke A. G. Leipzig.

     This booklet takes up various phases of the process of chromium plating. A historical sketch of the early development of the process is given. The writer then tells the properties and uses for chromium plate. A detailed account is given of the equipment recommended by the Langbein Pfanhauser works along with many helpful hints to the plater. Pfanhauser agrees with Müller's theory that chromium is deposited from hexavalent ion. Instructions are given in detail for preparing the work for plating, plating, stripping, polishing and for testing for corrosion resistance. The writer does not feel that the existing patents are of great import because of the work of Salzer and of Sargent.

96. 1927—G. F. Sager.
     A Study of the Production of Chromium Surfaces for Retarding the Corrosion of Nickel at High Temperatures.
     Master's Thesis: Rensselaer Polytechnic Institute.

     Sufficiently heavy chromium plates protect nickel against corrosion by sulphur dioxide. Surfaces of nickel-chromium, produced by diffusion of electrodeposited chromium or by chromizing mixtures, are however, superior, since they preserve their protective properties through considerable cold working.

     Attempts to roll duplex ingots into wire failed.

97. 1927—F. Sillers, Jr.
     The Crystal Structure of Electrodeposited Chromium.
     Trans. Am. Electrochem. Soc. 51: 301–307.

     X-ray crystal analysis of bright and dull chromium deposits show that it has a body-centered cubic structure, identical to that of chromium produced by the Goldschmidt process.

98. 1927—R. Schneidewind.
   A Study of Patents Dealing with the Electrodeposition of Chromium.
   Univ. of Mich. Eng. Research Bulletin #8.

99. 1927—H. E. Haring and W. P. Barrows.
   Electrodeposition of Chromium from Chromic Acid Baths.
   Bureau of Standards' Technologic Paper, No. 346.

   A detailed study is made of the chromic acid plating solution and of the conditions for its operation and control. The three principal types of chromic acid bath which have been developed during the past 70 years are shown to be identical, not only in initial behavior but also in ultimate composition. The recent commercial success of chromium plating is, therefore, attributed, not to any changes which have been effected in the composition of the bath, but to its more careful operation and control. It was found that minor improvements could be effected in the throwing power of chromic acid baths, but that there appears to be little possibility of materially improving this property which has hindered the more general adoption of chromium plating.

100. 1927—O. P. Watts.
   Anodes for Chromium Plating.
   Trans. Am. Electrochem. Soc. 52: 177–185.

   Lead is found to be the only satisfactory anode material. Iron is fairly good but goes into solution rapidly enough to make the bath inoperable. Other materials, such as Nicrome, stainless steel, silicon iron, nickel, etc., were tried but proved to be very poor. A table of comparative solubilities is given.

101. 1927—F. Adcock.
   Alloys of Iron Research. V. (Electrolytic).
   Preparation of Pure Chromium.
   Iron Steel Inst. (advance copy) 5–28.
   Engineering. 1323: 744–747.

   An electrolytic method for producing Cr, using Pb anodes and a solution containing 300 g. chromic acid and 10 g. H_2SO_4 per l., is described. Three types of apparatus are illustrated, the first involving a porous cell with Sn cathode, water-cooled, requiring 13 v. and giving a yield of 5 g. Cr per Kw.-hr. This metal was of high purity, but the crystals were insulated so as to be incapable of melting in a high-frequency induction furnace. The second apparatus with oxidized square steel bar cathodes, gave compact deposits, slightly contaminated with Fe; it required 4 to 4.5 v., and gave a yield of 22.6 g. Cr per kw.-hr. The third apparatus with a rotating cylindrical steel cathode, gave the same yield without contamination by Fe. The product contained H, and when melted *in vacuo* showed oxide inclusions, which were removed by heating in H at about 1550°. Liquid Cr dissolves its oxide, which is pptd. on cooling. The great hardness of ordinary electrodeposited Cr is due to a special condition, possibly associated with the presence of H.

102. 1927—H. J. French and H. K. Hershman.
Recent Experiments Relating to the Wear of Plug Gages.
Am. Soc. Steel Treating. 12: 921–945.

Results are given of tests made in a laboratory wear tester in gaging file-hard high-carbon steel, an aluminum "piston alloy" and a cast iron. Of the various gage metals investigated, chromium-plated gages showed the highest resistance to wear under conditions of metal-to-metal contact. Ammonia-treated chromium-aluminum steel, marketed under the name Nitralloy, was second in resistance to wear and much superior to the remainder of the group which showed variations, but no radical differences, in performance of the individual metals.

In tests made in file-hard high-carbon steel in the presence of a non-metallic abrasive, Stellite, a high-carbon high-chromium iron alloy and chromium-plated gages showed better resistance to wear than the customary high-carbon steels or the Nitralloy.

103. 1928—L. E. Grant and L. F. Grant.
Notes on the Hardness and Structure of Deposited Chromium.
Trans. Am. Electrochem. Soc. 53, Preprint.

The effect of current density and temperature on the hardness of Cr deposits was investigated. The hardest Cr deposits were obtained at relatively high c. ds. and the softest at low c. ds. At 30° deposits of the max. hardness could not be obtained at any c. d., while the hardest deposit at 60° was not any harder than that at 45°. At about 20 amp./sq. dm., the only current density that would yield a good deposit at all 3 temps., the hardest deposit was obtained at 45°. A temperature of 45° and the highest current density practicable were the best conditions found for the production of deposits of max. hardness. The presence of a network of cracks in some Cr deposits may be one cause of the deposits not protecting the base metal from corrosion.

104. 1928—E. M. Baker and W. L. Pinner.
Protective Value of Chromium Plate.
Jour. Am. Soc. Auto. Engrs. March.

The protective value of a composite coating depends largely upon the protection afforded by the underlying coats. Increase in the amount of chromium deposited upon nickel and copper, up to a thickness of 0.00001 to 0.00002 in. increases the protective value but a further increase of thickness up to 0.00027 in. of chromium decreases the protective value to almost the result obtained with no chromium at all.

105. 1928—V. Schischkin and Helen Gernet.
Contribution to the Theory of Electrolytic Deposition of Chromium from Chromic Acid Baths.
Zeit. f. Elektrochemie. 34: 57–62.

The electrolysis of CrO_3 solns. in which the relation of $Cr^{III}:Cr^{VI}$ = 1:35 is studied. A bright deposit is obtained at a current density of 10 amp./sq. dm. at about 45°. At temperatures around 10°, the deposit is thick and scaly, consisting chiefly of brown oxide. As the temperature rises to 20–30°, the deposit becomes dull and shows knobby growths under the microscope, while at 65° the dull deposit again appears. As the temperature rises the current efficiency falls. At 45°, if the current density becomes too high, (30 amp./sq. dm.) the deposit becomes dull and defective, although at this value of current, rotating the cathode at 200 r.p.m. gives a bright, uniform deposit. Increasing SO_4 concn. makes it possible to obtain a bright deposit at lower temperature and higher current density. With 28 g. Na_2SO_4 per l. (250 g. CrO_3/l.) a bright deposit is obtained at 25° and 14 amp./sq. dm.

The writers interpret phenomena observed in chromium deposition in the light of Liebreich's colloidal film theory. They offer an explanation for the production of dull and nodulized deposits by conceiving that the colloidal film is disturbed, particles thereof forming nuclei for roughnesses and trees.

106. 1928—R. Schneidewind, S. F. Urban, and R. C. Adams, Jr.
The Effect of Trivalent Chromium and Iron on Chromic-Acid Chromium Plating Baths.
Trans. Am. Electrochem. Soc. 53: preprint.
Given in full in the text of the bulletin.

107. 1928—R. Schneidewind and S. F. Urban.
Behavior of Plating Baths and Anodes During Electrodeposition of Chromium.
Trans. Am. Electrochem. Soc. 53: preprint.
Given in full in the text of the bulletin.

108. 1928—A. Siemens.
Present-day State of Chromium Plating Technique.
Zeit. f. Elektrochemie. 34: 264–269.

A historical sketch outlining the development of chromium plating. Special emphasis is placed upon Bureau of Standard Technologic Paper 346 by Haring and Barrows which is carefully reviewed.

109. 1928—E. Liebreich.
Patent Protection for Chromium Plating.
Oberflächentechnik. 5: 105–107.

The writer differs with the conclusions presented by Schneidewind (see 96). An account of some chromium plating researches is given. Carveth and Curry's deposits are described to have been poor and to have scaled badly. Liebreich ascribes this to a wrong SO_4 concentration in the bath. A chromic-acid bath upon use forms lower oxides of chromium which are necessary for metal deposition. The sulphate content of the bath should equal 1.2% of the weight of the chromic acid. Sargent's researches have done nothing but assemble a number of formulas for good baths.

110. 1928—H. S. Lukens.
The Influence of the Cathode on the Electrodeposition of Chromium.
Trans. Am. Electrochem. Soc. 53: preprint.

Cr may be deposited only within narrow limits of c. d. when electrolytic Ni cathodes are used, passive Ni being produced by electrodeposition. The influences of passive Ni, or Ni, Cu and Pb on the composition of solutions for the deposition of Cr are indicated. In general, the maximum amount of Cr^{+++} is produced at low c. ds., the least with Ni and the greatest with Pb. Cu yields practical deposits over the widest range of c. d. and Ni over the narrowest range. The observed effects are probably related to the respective H overvoltages and the rapidity with which the metal surfaces become covered with Cr. The amount of chromic salt is easily reduced when necessary by subjecting the solution to electrolysis, using a large Pb anode and a small cathode surrounded by a porous diaphragm. Excess SO_4 ions are removed by the addition of an emulsion of freshly pptd. $BaCrO_4$.

111. 1928—C. H. Eldridge.
Polishing and Buffing for Chromium Plating.
Metal Industry. 26: 258–259.

Better polish of the base metal is required if the article is to be chromeplated than if simply to be nickel plated. Chromium exaggerates surface imperfections. Buffing of nickel before chrome-plating should be done at high speed with low pressure; slow buffing leaves buff marks. Details are given for polishing pressed steel, forged steel and brass castings preparatory to nickel and chrome-plating.

Whale oil soap removes green Cr_2O_3 buffing compound; electrolytic cleaning will not. A brown Cr_2O_3 compound is softer than the green and is useful for buffing plumbing fixtures.

PART V

APPENDICES

APPENDIX A. A SUMMARY OF THE HISTORY OF THE DEVELOPMENT OF CHROMIUM-PLATING PROCESSES

APPENDIX B. TABLES OF DATA ON ORIGINAL RESEARCH

SUMMARY OF HISTORICAL DEVELOPMENT OF CHROMIUM PLATING

INVESTIGATOR	YEAR	ORIGINAL REFERENCE NUMBER OF REFERENCE IN BIBLIOGRAPHY IN PARENTHESIS	COMPOSITION OF BATH (CATHOLYTE)	CATHODE DEPOSIT	CATHODE CURRENT DENSITY amp/dcm^2	VOLTAGE	CATHODE CURRENT EFFICIENCY per cent	TEMPERATURE °C.	DIAPHRAGM	ANODES	REMARKS
Junot	1852 (1849?)	Brit. P. 1183 (1853) (1)	Cr dissolved in a double chloride of Na and NH_4	Cr	—	—	—	30-40	—	C	
Bunsen	1854	Pogg. Ann. 91: 119 (2)	Concentrated solution of $CrCl_2$ with some $CrCl_3$ present	Cr	65	—	—	100	Yes	Pt	
Geuther	1856	Liebig. Ann. 99: 314 (3)	Solution of CrO_3 prepared from H_2SO_4 and $K_2Cr_2O_7$	Cr	High	4 Bunsen Cells	35-46	—	No	Pt	SO_4= impurity probably present
Buff	1857	Liebig. Ann. 101: 1 (4)	Solution of pure CrO_3	H_2	High	4 Bunsen Cells	—	—	No	Pt	
Morges	1878	Comptes Rendus 87: 15 (7)	Dilute solution of CrO_3	$Cr_2(CrO_4)_3$	—	—	—	—	No	—	
Bartoli and Papasogli	1883	Gazz. chim. Ital. 13: 47 (9)	Solution of CrO_3	Cr	—	—	—	—	No	C	Deposit very tenacious and brilliant
Slater	1884	Brit P. 5245 (10)	Solution containing Cr and other metal chlorides	Cr alloys	—	0.5 or more	—	65	No	Cr alloy	

Name	Date	Patent	Electrolyte	Cr form						Notes
Placet and Bonnet	1890 to 1896	U. S. P. 526114 (1894)	Solution containing 10–20 or more grams per liter of CrO_3 + addition agents such as sulphuric, benzoic, hydrochloric acids or their salts	Cr	—	—	—	—	No	Pb
		(12)	100–150 g./l. $Cr_2(SO_4)_3$ or Cr-alum. Oxalic acid optional	Cr	—	—	—	—	—	Pb
			Cr''' salts + Dextrin and alkali and alkaline earth chlorides	Cr	—	30–40	—	—	—	Pb
Marino	1896	U.S.P. 607646 (1898) (14)	Solution of $CrCl_3 + CaSO_4$	Cr	—	—	—	—	—	—
Moeller and Street	1898	Brit. P. 18743 D. R. P. 105847 (16)	Equal parts of H_2O, Cr-alum, and neutral Na_2SO_4 Anolyte = H_2SO_4	Cr	40	—	30	70	Yes	Pb
Boehringer and Sons	1899	D. R. P. 115463 (18)	500 g. $Cr_2(SO_4)_3$ 500 g. H_2O 250 g. H_2SO_4	Cr'' salts	10–15	—	—	—	—	Pb
			100 g. of a concentrated $Cr_2(SO_4)_3$ solution diluted to 600 cc. and saturated with NaCl and Na_2SO_4	No Cr Trace of oxide	20–30	—	—	30–80	Yes	Pb cathode
Le Blanc	—	Book: Die Darstellung des Chroms.	15 g. Cr-alum 15 g. $K_2Cr_2O_7$ 100 g. H_2O	Trace of Cr	20–30	—	—	30–80	Yes	—
			15 g. Cr-alum 15 g. $NaHSO_4$ 100 g. H_2O	Trace of Cr	20–30	—	—	30–80	Yes	—
			15 g. Cr-alum 15 g. NH_4F 10 g. HCl 100 g. H_2O	Trace of Cr	20–30	—	—	30–80	Yes	—

INVESTIGATOR	YEAR	ORIGINAL REFERENCE. NUMBER OF REFERENCE IN BIBLIOGRAPHY IN PARENTHESIS	COMPOSITION OF BATH (CATHOLYTE)	CATHODE DEPOSIT	CATHODE CURRENT DENSITY amp/dcm^2	VOLTAGE	CATHODE CURRENT EFFICIENCY per cent	TEMPERATURE °C.	DIAPHRAGM	ANODES	REMARKS
Cowper-Coles	1900	Chem. News. 81: 16 (22)	25 per cent solution of $CrCl_3$ acidulated with HCl	Cr	4.5–5.5	4	—	75	—	Pb	
Férée	1901	Bull. Soc. Chim. Paris. [3] 25: 617 (25)	740 g. H_2O 160 g. $CrCl_3$ crystals 100 g. HCl	99.8 per cent pure Cr	15	8	45	—	—	—	
Férée	1901	Bull. Soc. Chim. Paris. [3] 25: 617 (25)	266.5 g. $CrCl_3 \cdot 6H_2O$ 233.5 g. KCl H_2O to make 1 liter	Silvery-white Cr	15	8	45	—	—	—	
		Bull. Soc. Chim. Paris. [3] 25: 620	Neutral $CrCl_3$ solutions 160 grams per liter	Cr_2O_3	High	—	—	—	—	—	
			Acidified solutions of $CrCl_3$	H_2	2.5	—	—	—	—	—	Hg cathode
Goldschmidt	1901	Z. f. Elektrochemie 7: 656 Discussion	Solutions of chromic salts acidified with HCl or CH_3COOH	Cr	10–15	—	—	—	—	—	
Neumann and Glaser	1901	Z. f. Elektrochemie 7: 656 (26)	$Cr_2(SO_4)_3$ solution 65–85 grams per liter	Cr	12–20	—	84.6	20	Yes	Pt	At best conditions
Neumann and Glaser	1901	Z. f. Elektrochemie 7: 656 (26)	Other $CrCl_3$, Cr-acetate and Cr-sulphate baths	Cr oxides or Cr depending on current density	Up to 38	—	—	—	Yes	Pt	
P. Marino Q. Marino G. Marino A. Ratchkowsky	1901	Brit. P. 15427 (1902)	A complex phosphate-chloride bath	Cr	—	—	—	—	—	—	Vague

Investigator	Year	Reference	Solution	Cr'' salts						Anode	Remarks
Le Blanc	—	Book: Das Chrom und seine Verbindungen (30 and 34)	200 g. $Cr_2(SO_4)_3$ anhyd. 200 g. H_2O 100 g. H_2SO_4	Cr'' salts	10–15	—	—	30–80	Yes	—	—
Carveth and Mott	1905	Jour. Phys. Chem. 9: 231–256. (31)	Solution of $CrCl_3$ containing 100 g./l. of metal	Cr	Up to 70	—	Up to 30	22	Yes	Pt	—
	1905		Solution of $Cr_2(SO_4)_3$ containing 83 g./l. of metal	Cr	Up to 130	—	Up to 70	20–30	Yes	Pt	—
Carveth and Curry	1905	Jour. Phys. Chem. 9: 353–380. Also Trans. Am. Electrochem. Soc. 7: 115ff. (32)	14.28 per cent solution of CrO_3 + 1 per cent H_2SO_4. Other acids and salts were substituted	Cr	125	—	35–50	20	No	Pt	Deposit did not peel when cathode was twisted and distorted
Salzer	1907	D. R. P. 221472 (1910) U. S. P. 900597 (1908) (36)	CrO_3 + Cr_2O_3 in 2:1 ratio trace of H_2SO_4 may be added	Cr	2–5	—	—	20	Yes or No	Fe_3O_4 Pb Pt	—
	1909	D. R. P. 225769 (1910) (37)	CrO_3 13 per cent / Cr_2O_3 11 per cent / $Cr_2(SO_4)_3$ 12 per cent / H_2O remainder	Cr	2–5	—	—	20	No	—	—
Baum	1912	Brit. P. 16865 (1913) (41)	10 per cent solution of CrO_3 + 1 per cent of some acid such as boric	Cr	—	—	—	—	—	—	—
Askenasy and Revai	1913	Z. f. Elektrochemie 19: 362 (42)	Solution of CrO_3 + H_2SO_4 or similar impurity	Cr	—	—	—	—	—	—	—
Sargent	1920	Trans. Am. Electrochem. Soc. 37: 275–292 (44)	Solution containing 25 per cent CrO_3 + 0.3 per cent $Cr_2(SO_4)_3$	Cr	10	—	30	20	No	Pt or Pb	—

INVESTIGATOR	YEAR	ORIGINAL REFERENCE. NUMBER OF REFERENCE IN BIBLIOGRAPHY IN PARENTHESIS	COMPOSITION OF BATH (CATHOLYTE)	CATHODE DEPOSIT	CATHODE CURRENT DENSITY amp/dcm^2	VOLTAGE	CATHODE CURRENT EFFICIENCY per cent	TEMPERATURE °C.	DIAPHRAGM	ANODES	REMARKS
Liebreich	1920	D. R. P. 398054 (1924) (45)	Solution containing CrO_3 + Cr'''	Cr	Under 45	—	—	20	No	Pb	Later articles and patents describe $SO_4^=$ impurity
Grube	1921	U. S. P. 1496845 (1924) (48)	250 g./l. CrO_3 3 g./l. $Cr_2(SO_4)_3$ 6 g./l. $Cr(OH)_3$	Cr	—	—	—	—	No	Pb	
Pierce and Humphries	1924	U. S. P. 1545196 (1925)	Essentially 240 g./l. CrO_3 3.8 g./l. $Cr_2(SO_4)_3$ 30–40 cc./l. NH_4OH	Cr	1.5 to 14.0	—	—	20	No	Pb	
Haring	1925	Chem. and Met. Eng. 32: 692, 756 (82)	250 g./l. CrO_3 3 g./l. $Cr_2(SO_4)_3$ 7 g./l. Cr-carbonate	Cr	C. D. and yield dependent on temperature				No	Pb	
Fink	1925	U. S. P. 1581188 (1926) (81)	250 g./l. CrO_3 1 to 5 g./l. $SO_4^=$ or similar anion	Cr	4 to 16	—	—	15 to 40	No	Pb	Stronger or weaker solutions may be used
Haring and Barrows	1927	Bureau of Standards T. P. 346 (99)	250 g./l. CrO_3 2.5 g./l. $SO_4^=$	Cr	C. D. and yield dependent on temperature				No	Pb Fe	

APPENDIX B
TABLES OF DATA ON ORIGINAL RESEARCH

TABLE 1
Current Density-Current Efficiency Relationship of a 235 g./l. Chromic-Acid Bath at 15°C.

Ratio $\dfrac{Cr^{VI}}{SO_4} = 50$

CATHODE CURRENT DENSITY		CURRENT EFFICIENCY	APPEARANCE
$amp./dcm^2.$	$amp./ft^2.$	per cent	
9.2	86	27.4	4-*
23.2	216	37.8	4
26.8	249	39.8	4
29.1	270	39.7	4
33.7	313	41.1	4
34.2	318	40.7	4
41.3	384	42.4	4
43.4	403	43.4	4

* There was a six second lag before plating began. This is a sign that the lower current-density limit was approached.

TABLE 2
Current Density-Current Efficiency Relationship of a 235 g./l. Chromic-Acid Bath at 25°C.

Ratio $\dfrac{Cr^{VI}}{SO_4} = 50$

CATHODE CURRENT DENSITY		CURRENT EFFICIENCY	APPEARANCE
$amp./dcm^2.$	$amp./ft^2.$	per cent	
3.0	28	10.5	3
4.7	43	12.8	3
5.7	53	13.9	3
8.3	77	19.6	3+
10.7	99	22.0	3+
10.9	101	22.8	3+
14.4	134	24.2	4
17.8	165	24.7	4
18.5	172	25.2	4
19.2	178	28.9	4
22.5	209	29.9	4
23.7	220	29.0	4
33.9	315	31.3	4
37.5	350	36.9	4
45.8	426	38.5	4
70.0	650	39.3	4

TABLE 3
Current Density-Current Efficiency Relationship of a 235 g./l. Chromic-Acid Bath at 45°C

Ratio $\dfrac{Cr^{VI}}{SO_4} = 50$

CATHODE CURRENT DENSITY		CURRENT EFFICIENCY	APPEARANCE
amp./dcm².	amp./ft².	per cent	
6.4	59		3–*
7.7	68	9.7	3
12.3	114	14.3	3
15.6	145	16.1	3
17.3	161	15.9	3
20.2	188	16.9	3
28.8	268	19.6	3+
36.2	336	21.9	3+
48.5	451	24.4	4
71.7	667	26.6	4

* Lag of six seconds before plating began.

TABLE 4
Current Density-Current Efficiency Relationship of a 235 g./l. Chromic-Acid Bath at 60°C.

Ratio $\dfrac{Cr^{VI}}{SO_4} = 50$

CATHODE CURRENT DENSITY		CURRENT EFFICIENCY	APPEARANCE
amp./dcm².	amp./ft².	per cent	
12.7	118	11.9	3
17.2	160	14.8	3
37.5	348	16.5	3
45.6	425	18.1	3
57.6	535	19.3	3+
64.7	601	19.1	3+
78.8	733	19.7	3+
88.3	820	20.4	3+
95.6	888	21.8	3+
111.0	1,030	22.7	3+
120.6	1,120	23.0	3+
154.0	1,430	24.5	4
196.0	1,820	25.4	4

TABLE 5

CURRENT DENSITY-CURRENT EFFICIENCY RELATIONSHIP OF A 235 g./l. CHROMIC-ACID BATH AT 75°C.

Ratio $\dfrac{Cr^{VI}}{SO_4} = 50$

CATHODE CURRENT DENSITY		CURRENT EFFICIENCY	APPEARANCE
amp./dcm².	*amp./ft²*.	*per cent*	
34.5	320	9.9	3—
35.8	332	10.7	3—
38.2	355	11.0	3—
46.9	436	12.0	3
52.0	483	12.9	3
59.0	548	13.2	3
92.8	861	15.5	3
101.5	945	15.3	3
180.2	1,674	19.4	3*
198.2	1,845	18.5	3*
326.0	3,030	16.7	3*
465.0	4,320	25.6	4*

* Trees were formed on specimen. The fragility of the trees may apparently tend to lower the current efficiency below its true value.

TABLE 6

CURRENT DENSITY-CURRENT EFFICIENCY RELATIONSHIP OF A 235 g./l. CHROMIC-ACID BATH AT 85°C.

Ratio $\dfrac{Cr^{VI}}{SO_4} = 50$

CATHODE CURRENT DENSITY		CURRENT EFFICIENCY	APPEARANCE
amp./dcm².	*amp./ft²*.	*per cent*	
34.8	324	7.7	3—
58.5	554	12.6	3
67.6	628	12.8	3
72.0	670	13.7	3
80.0	743	13.8	3
87.8	816	10.3	3
88.2	820	13.8	3
90.6	843	13.0	3
96.0	894	14.5	3
139.7	1,298	15.7	3*
167.0	1,553	17.2	3*
397.0	3,690	21.8	3+*

* Trees were formed on specimen. The fragility of the trees may apparently tend to lower the current efficiency below its true value.

TABLE 7
Bright Plating Range on Copper Cathodes at 25°C.
CrO$_3$ Concentration 235 grams per liter. Maximum thickness of deposit 0.0007 mm. (0.00003 in.)

SO$_4$ CONCENTRATION	RATIO $\frac{Cr^{VI}}{SO_4}$	LOWER LIMIT		UPPER LIMIT	
g./l.		amp./dcm².	amp./ft².	amp./dcm².	amp./ft².
1.11	110.0	2.4	22.0	4.0	37.0
1.71	71.3	2.1	20.0	6.9	65.0
2.03	60.0	2.0	19.0	7.5	70.0
2.19	55.7	2.0	19.0	7.5	70.0
2.42	50.0	2.2	21.0	7.8	73.0
3.05	40.0	3.2	30.0	7.8	73.0
3.90	31.2	4.5	42.0	8.6	80.0
5.07	24.0	6.4	60.0	9.6	90.0
8.35	14.6	11.8	110.0	13.9	130.0

TABLE 8
Bright Plating Range on Copper Cathodes at 45°C.
CrO$_3$ Concentration 235 grams per liter. Maximum thickness of deposit 0.0007 mm. (0.00003 in.)

SO$_4$ CONCENTRATION	RATIO $\frac{Cr^{VI}}{SO_4}$	LOWER LIMIT		UPPER LIMIT	
g./l.		amp./dcm².	amp./ft².	amp./dcm².	amp./ft².
1.11	110.0	6.9	65.0	11.8	110.0
1.71	71.3	4.8	45.0	21.4	200.0
2.42	50.0	5.4	50.0	16.1	150.0
3.05	40.0	5.9	55.0	15.0	140.0
3.90	31.2	6.4	60.0	17.1	160.0
5.07	24.0	7.5	70.0	18.7	175.0
8.35	15.2	16.1	150.0	24.6	230.0

TABLE 9
Bright Plating Range on Copper Cathodes at 60°C.
CrO₃ Concentration 235 grams per liter. Maximum thickness of deposit 0.0007 mm. (0.00003 in.)

SO₄ CONCENTRATION	RATIO $\frac{Cr^{VI}}{SO_4}$	LOWER LIMIT		UPPER LIMIT	
g./l.		amp./dcm².	amp./ft².	amp./dcm².	amp./ft².
1.11	110.0	10.7	100	64.2	600
1.71	71.3	10.7	100	74.9	700
2.16	56.5	11.8	110	64.2	600
2.42	50.0	11.2	105	53.5	500
3.05	40.0	10.7	100	42.9	400
3.90	31.2	11.8	110	40.1	375
5.07	24.0	16.1	150	48.1	450
5.96	20.5	21.4	200	58.8	550
8.35	15.2	42.8	400	61.5	575

TABLE 10
Current Density-Current Efficiency Relationship of a 235 g./l. Chromic-Acid Bath at 25°C.
Ratio $\frac{Cr^{VI}}{SO_4}$ = 102

CATHODE CURRENT DENSITY		CURRENT EFFICIENCY	APPEARANCE
amp./dcm².	amp./ft².	per cent	
11.1	103	23.5	4
10.8	100	23.7	4
10.6	98	22.9	4
20.5	190	29.1	4
20.7	192	31.5	4
32.7	304	34.5	4
32.1	298	36.2	4
34.4	319	35.5	4
55.5	515	38.0	4
58.1	540	38.5	4
59.7	555	39.1	4

TABLE 11
Current Density-Current Efficiency Relationship of a 235 g./l. Chromic-Acid Bath at 45°C.

$$\text{Ratio } \frac{Cr^{VI}}{SO_4} = 102$$

CATHODE CURRENT DENSITY		CURRENT EFFICIENCY	APPEARANCE
$amp./dcm^2$.	$amp./ft^2$.	per cent	
11.2	104	11.1	3
11.3	105	11.1	3
12.4	115	12.4	3
21.5	199	14.5	3
21.8	202	13.1	3
22.6	210	15.7	3+
32.7	303	16.1	3+
31.2	290	15.3	3+
32.4	301	17.2	3+
43.5	403	16.0	4
51.8	480	18.1	4
48.0	445	16.4	4

TABLE 12
Current Density-Current Efficiency Relationship of a 235 g./l. Chromic-Acid Bath at 60°C.

$$\text{Ratio } \frac{Cr^{VI}}{SO_4} = 102$$

CATHODE CURRENT DENSITY		CURRENT EFFICIENCY	APPEARANCE
$amp./dcm^2$.	$amp./ft^2$.	per cent	
10.4	96	7.4	3−
10.6	98	7.2	3−
10.5	97	7.4	3−
23.0	213	10.3	3
20.7	192	10.1	3
24.9	231	11.4	3
33.8	314	12.4	3
35.2	327	11.5	3
34.2	317	11.7	3
53.9	500	14.3	3
48.7	452	12.4	3
49.1	456	11.8	3

TABLE 13
Current Density-Current Efficiency Relationship of a 235 g./l. Chromic-Acid Bath at 25°C.

Ratio $\dfrac{Cr^{VI}}{SO_4} = 64.5$

CATHODE CURRENT DENSITY		CURRENT EFFICIENCY	APPEARANCE
amp./dcm².	amp./ft².	per cent	
10.6	98	22.4	4
10.6	98	23.3	4
10.8	101	23.3	4
20.7	192	31.1	4
20.6	191	29.9	4
22.2	206	30.5	4
32.1	298	36.2	4
31.8	295	36.2	4
31.4	291	36.0	4
52.3	485	40.3	4
51.2	475	41.1	4
53.5	496	39.9	4

TABLE 14
Current Density-Current Efficiency Relationship of a 235 g./l. Chromic-Acid Bath at 45°C.

Ratio $\dfrac{Cr^{VI}}{SO_4} = 64.5$

CATHODE CURRENT DENSITY		CURRENT EFFICIENCY	APPEARANCE
amp./dcm².	amp./ft².	per cent	
10.0	93	12.6	3
10.5	97	13.1	3
10.6	98	13.2	3
22.8	210	18.0	3+
21.0	195	16.5	3+
30.9	287	20.4	4
32.6	303	20.6	4
31.8	295	20.5	4
51.2	475	23.1	4
50.9	472	23.7	4
55.2	512	25.7	4

TABLE 15
Current Density-Current Efficiency Relationship of a 235 g./l. Chromic-Acid Bath at 60°C.

Ratio $\dfrac{Cr^{VI}}{SO_4} = 64.5$

CATHODE CURRENT DENSITY		CURRENT EFFICIENCY	APPEARANCE
amp./dcm².	amp./ft².	per cent	
11.2	104	8.9	3
12.8	119	8.4	3
14.2	132	10.3	3
23.0	213	11.5	3
23.0	213	12.3	3
23.0	213	13.0	3
33.1	307	14.7	3
30.8	286	14.2	3
33.0	306	15.2	3
53.9	500	17.4	3+
53.9	500	16.4	3+
53.9	500	16.6	3+

TABLE 16
Current Density-Current Efficiency Relationship of a 235 g./l. Chromic-Acid Bath at 25°C.

Ratio $\dfrac{Cr^{VI}}{SO_4} = 46.3$

CATHODE CURRENT DENSITY		CURRENT EFFICIENCY	APPEARANCE
amp./dcm².	amp./ft².	per cent	
10.5	97	22.2	4
11.0	102	21.8	4
11.4	106	23.0	4
21.5	200	29.1	4
24.0	223	33.1	4
23.2	215	32.2	4
32.0	297	34.3	4
31.9	296	36.2	4
28.0	260	33.1	4
50.9	472	39.7	4
57.8	536	41.8	4
51.2	475	41.7	4

TABLE 17
Current Density-Current Efficiency Relationship of a 235 g./l. Chromic-Acid Bath at 45°C.

$$\text{Ratio } \frac{Cr^{VI}}{SO_4} = 46.3$$

CATHODE CURRENT DENSITY		CURRENT EFFICIENCY	APPEARANCE
$amp./dcm^2$.	$amp./ft^2$.	per cent	
11.7	109	13.9	3
12.2	113	13.6	3
12.6	117	15.1	3
21.6	200	18.7	3+
19.9	185	18.6	3
21.2	197	18.7	3+
36.0	334	23.7	4
36.4	338	22.7	4
35.6	331	23.3	4
51.2	475	25.6	4
52.8	490	26.6	4

TABLE 18
Current Density-Current Efficiency Relationship of a 235 g./l. Chromic-Acid Bath at 60°C.

$$\text{Ratio } \frac{Cr^{VI}}{SO_4} = 46.3$$

CATHODE CURRENT DENSITY		CURRENT EFFICIENCY	APPEARANCE
$amp./dcm^2$.	$amp./ft^2$.	per cent	
9.6	89	8.3	3
10.3	95	9.6	3
19.9	185	13.1	3
23.2	215	13.4	3
19.1	177	13.1	3
35.8	332	15.7	3
39.6	367	17.1	3+
31.8	295	15.2	3
47.1	437	17.1	3+
57.4	532	17.6	3+
59.8	555	17.8	3+

TABLE 19
CURRENT DENSITY-CURRENT EFFICIENCY RELATIONSHIP OF A 235 g./l. CHROMIC-ACID BATH AT 60°C.

Ratio $\dfrac{Cr^{VI}}{SO_4} = 30.0$

CATHODE CURRENT DENSITY		CURRENT EFFICIENCY	APPEARANCE
amp./dcm².	amp./ft².	per cent	
12.4	115		Below plating range—incomplete plate
15.3	142	9.5	2
19.7	183	10.8	2
20.3	189	11.1	3 — (milky)
42.0	390	16.0	3
38.3	356	15.3	3
39.2	364	15.3	3
34.7	322	14.7	3
81.6	758	20.9	3+ almost 3
81.4	756	18.3	3+ almost 3

TABLE 20
CURRENT DENSITY-CURRENT EFFICIENCY RELATIONSHIP OF A 235 g./l. CHROMIC-ACID BATH AT 25°C.

Ratio $\dfrac{Cr^{VI}}{SO_4} = 18.5$

CATHODE CURRENT DENSITY		CURRENT EFFICIENCY	APPEARANCE
amp./dcm².	amp./ft².	per cent	
11.0	102	12.2	Milky, voltage pulsated
12.0	111	14.2	Milky, voltage pulsated
22.0	204	25.8	3+
20.3	188	23.4	3+
22.4	208	24.9	3+
34.0	315	33.2	4
33.0	306	29.5	4
35.4	329	34.1	4
53.5	496	39.6	4
56.2	522	40.5	4
51.0	473	39.2	4

TABLE 21
CURRENT DENSITY-CURRENT EFFICIENCY RELATIONSHIP OF A 235 g./l. CHROMIC-ACID BATH AT 45°C.

$$\text{Ratio } \frac{Cr^{VI}}{SO_4} = 18.5$$

CATHODE CURRENT DENSITY		CURRENT EFFICIENCY	APPEARANCE
amp./dcm².	amp./ft².	per cent	
10.5	97		No plate, below plating range
22.8	212	11.5	3 — incomplete plate
21.6	201	11.5	3 — incomplete plate
22.8	212	14.9	3
31.6	293	17.2	3+
33.6	312	17.2	3+
34.0	316	18.0	3+
50.9	472	23.4	4
55.5	515	24.9	4
54.6	507	25.1	4

TABLE 22
CURRENT DENSITY-CURRENT EFFICIENCY RELATIONSHIP OF A 235 g./l. CHROMIC-ACID BATH AT 60°C.

$$\text{Ratio } \frac{Cr^{VI}}{SO_4} = 18.5$$

CATHODE CURRENT DENSITY		CURRENT EFFICIENCY	APPEARANCE
amp./dcm².	amp./ft².	per cent	
34.3	318	11.7	3 —
38.6	358	13.5	3 — almost 3
53.5	497	17.1	3+
53.9	500	18.8	3+
55.6	516	16.6	3+
99.6	925	21.0	4
99.2	920	20.8	4
100.0	927	21.0	4
124.6	1157	23.1	4
134.1	1245	25.3	4
124.4	1155	22.9	4

TABLE 23
Current Density-Current Efficiency Relationship of a 117 g./l. Chromic-Acid Bath at 25°C.

$$\text{Ratio } \frac{Cr^{VI}}{SO_4} = 102$$

CATHODE CURRENT DENSITY		CURRENT EFFICIENCY	APPEARANCE
amp./dcm².	amp./ft².	per cent	
5.6	52	15.8	3+
5.0	46	14.9	3+
5.0	46	15.7	3+
10.3	94	24.1	3+
11.4	106	23.4	3+
9.4	87	20.9	3+
20.4	189	28.1	4
19.5	181	28.0	4
18.1	168	28.7	4
31.7	295	30.3	4
30.0	278	30.5	4
31.0	288	31.1	4
53.9	500	33.4°	4
45.8	425	31.7	4
47.0	437	32.0	4

Bright range on copper, maximum thickness of deposit 0.0007 mm., from 2.7 to 4.3 amp./dcm². (25 to 40 amp./ft².).

TABLE 24
Current Density-Current Efficiency Relationship of a 117 g./l. Chromic-Acid Bath at 25°C.

$$\text{Ratio } \frac{Cr^{VI}}{SO_4} = 64.5$$

CATHODE CURRENT DENSITY		CURRENT EFFICIENCY	APPEARANCE
amp./dcm².	amp./ft².	per cent	
5.4	50	16.4	3+
5.0	46	16.3	3+
10.1	94	22.0	3+
9.4	86	21.7	3+
8.7	81	20.5	3+
21.1	196	29.7	4
21.5	200	28.9	4
32.3	300	34.1	4
27.8	258	31.9	4
28.3	263	39.8	4
50.0	465	35.1	4
52.3	485	35.3	4
55.6	516	35.4	4

Bright range on copper, maximum thickness of deposit 0.0007 mm., from 3.1 to 4.7 amp./dcm². (29 to 43 amp./ft².).

TABLE 25
Current Density-Current Efficiency Relationship of a 117 g./l. Chromic-Acid Bath at 25°C.

Ratio $\dfrac{Cr^{VI}}{SO_4} = 46.3$

CATHODE CURRENT DENSITY		CURRENT EFFICIENCY	APPEARANCE
amp./dcm².	amp./ft².	per cent	
5.0	46	16.5	3+
9.9	92	22.3	3+
9.8	91	22.1	3+
10.7	99	23.1	3+
19.8	184	30.3	4
20.1	187	30.1	4
30.0	278	34.5	4
30.6	284	34.5	4
31.6	294	35.5	4
55.0	510	39.2	4
51.7	480	38.1	4

Bright range on copper, maximum thickness of deposit 0.0007 mm., from 2.9 to 4.0 amp./dcm². (27 to 37 amp./ft².).

TABLE 26
Current Density-Current Efficiency Relationship of a 117 g./l. Chromic-Acid Bath at 25°C.

Ratio $\dfrac{Cr^{VI}}{SO_4} = 18.5$

CATHODE CURRENT DENSITY		CURRENT EFFICIENCY	APPEARANCE	
amp./dcm².	amp./ft².	per cent		
5.3	49	2.1	3	
5.9	55	5.2	3	
5.4	50	2.5	3	
10.7	99	18.4	3+	brown stain—wiped off easily
10.6	98	17.9	3+	
10.5	97	17.5	3+	
21.3	198	27.6	4	heavy brown stain—adherent
21.5	200	26.2	4	
21.6	201	28.3	4	
30.5	283	29.4	4	heavy brown stain—adherent
31.0	288	30.9	4	
33.2	308	29.6	4	
55.0	510	31.0	4	tendency to peel
56.2	522	33.2	4	
50.7	472	31.3	4	

At greater current densities the deposit peeled badly.
Bright range on copper, maximum thickness of deposit 0.0007 mm., from 4.5 to 6.1 amp./dcm². (42 to 57 amp./ft².).

TABLE 27
Current Density-Current Efficiency Relationship of a 345 g./l. Chromic-Acid Bath at 25°C.

Ratio $\dfrac{Cr^{VI}}{SO_4} = 102$

CATHODE CURRENT DENSITY		CURRENT EFFICIENCY	APPEARANCE
amp./dcm².	amp./ft².	per cent	
4.7	44	13.3	3
5.0	46	13.8	3
11.4	106	21.7	3+
11.0	102	23.6	3+
12.9	120	24.0	3+
22.8	212	30.0	4
23.5	218	29.3	4
23.3	216	30.5	4
39.0	362	33.3	4
35.5	330	32.9	4
28.4	264	30.7	4
57.8	537	36.9	4
60.0	555	37.4	4
46.5	431	35.0	4

Bright range on copper, maximum thickness of deposit 0.0007 mm., from 2.1 to 5.0 amp./dcm². (20 to 47 amp./ft².).

TABLE 28
Current Density-Current Efficiency Relationship of a 345 g./l. Chromic-Acid Bath at 25°C.

Ratio $\dfrac{Cr^{VI}}{SO_4} = 64.5$

CATHODE CURRENT DENSITY		CURRENT EFFICIENCY	APPEARANCE
amp./dcm².	amp./ft².	per cent	
4.2	39	13.0	3
4.6	43	13.3	3
9.7	90	20.2	3+
10.6	98	22.2	3+
21.8	202	39.8	4
35.2	327	35.1	4
30.3	281	34.2	4
52.0	482	40.4	4
57.2	532	42.8	4

Bright range on copper, maximum thickness of deposit 0.0007 mm., from 2.4 to 5.4 amp./dcm². (22 to 50 amp./ft².).

TABLE 29

CURRENT DENSITY-CURRENT EFFICIENCY RELATIONSHIP OF A 345 g./l. CHROMIC-ACID BATH AT 25°C.

Ratio $\dfrac{Cr^{VI}}{SO_4} = 46.3$

CATHODE CURRENT DENSITY		CURRENT EFFICIENCY	APPEARANCE
amp./dcm².	amp./ft².	per cent	
4.7	45	11.0	3
8.2	76	17.0	3+
10.5	98	20.5	3+
12.1	112	23.0	3+
22.5	209	29.3	4
30.6	284	32.1	4
30.7	285	31.1	4
54.7	508	38.9	4
53.3	495	38.7	4
110.5	1025	45.8	4
111.5	1135	46.4	4

Bright range on copper, maximum thickness of deposit 0.0007 mm., from 3.4 to 6.5 amp./dcm². (32 to 60 amp./ft².).

TABLE 30

CURRENT DENSITY-CURRENT EFFICIENCY RELATIONSHIP OF A 345 g./l. CHROMIC-ACID BATH AT 25° C.

Ratio $\dfrac{Cr^{VI}}{SO_4} = 18.5$

CATHODE CURRENT DENSITY		CURRENT EFFICIENCY	APPEARANCE	
amp./dcm².	amp./ft².	per cent		
5.4	50		—	below plating range
12.7	118	8.1	3	milky
13.5	125	10.5	3	
24.4	226	21.8	3+	
29.2	271	26.0	4	
29.6	275	27.0	4	
58.6	545	39.3	4	
57.6	535	39.1	4	

Bright range on copper, maximum thickness of deposit 0.0007 mm., from 11.6 to 14.7 amp./dcm². (108 to 137 amp./ft².).

CPSIA information can be obtained at www.ICGtesting.com
Printed in the USA
LVOW04s1954231214

420155LV00025B/482/P